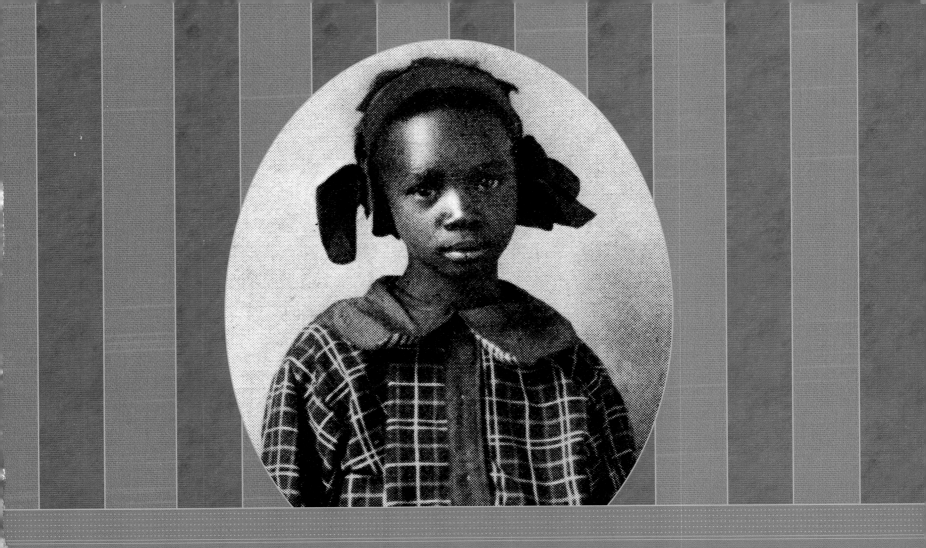

SEARCHING FOR
SARAH RECTOR
THE RICHEST BLACK GIRL IN AMERICA

Library of Congress Cataloging-in-Publication Data

Bolden, Tonya.
Searching for Sarah Rector / Tonya Bolden.
pages cm
Includes bibliographical references and index.
ISBN 978-1-4197-0846-6
1. Rector, Sarah, 1902— —Juvenile literature. 2. African American women—Oklahoma—Creek County—Biography—Juvenile literature. 3. African Americans—Oklahoma—Creek County—Biography—Juvenile literature. 4. Women millionaires—Oklahoma—Creek County—Biography—Juvenile literature. 5. Millionaires—Oklahoma—Creek County—Biography—Juvenile literature. 6. Creek Indians—Oklahoma—Creek County—Biography—Juvenile literature. 7. Petroleum industry and trade—Oklahoma—History—20th century—Juvenile literature. 8. Creek County (Okla.)—Biography. I. Title.
F702.C85B65 2014
976.6'84053092—dc23
[B]
2012039254

Text copyright © 2014 Tonya Bolden
Book design by Maria T. Middleton

Printed and bound in China
10 9 8 7 6 5 4 3

Abrams Books for Young Readers are available at special discounts when purchased in quantity for premiums and promotions as well as fundraising or educational use. Special editions can also be created to specification. For details, contact specialsales@abramsbooks.com or the address below.

THE ART OF BOOKS SINCE 1949
115 West 18th Street
New York, NY 10011
www.abramsbooks.com

CONTENTS

Sarah Rector, at twelve years old.

PROLOGUE

"DEAR SIR: AFTER READING YOUR ACCOUNT OF THE LITTLE GIRL, Sarah Rector, I am writing to state that I heartily approve that part of your statement which says she 'cannot be hid.'" That's how John A. Melby of Gary, Indiana, began his letter to R. S. Abbott, publisher of the *Chicago Defender*, a weekly paper. Melby's letter was dated March 15, 1914.

The day before, the *Defender* had run a front-page story on twelve-year-old Sarah Rector, raising the frightening possibility of a kidnapping. It punctuated the piece at points with the question "Where is Sarah Rector?"

Melby urged Abbott to do whatever it took to solve the mystery—even hire a detective "to get at the facts."

Why were Melby and the *Defender* so worked up over Sarah Rector? Would they have spent the same amount of ink on any other girl—or boy—gone missing?

We'd like to think so, but we know that Sarah wasn't just any girl. She was being ballyhooed as the richest black girl in America—some said in the world. The scuttlebutt was that Sarah had an income of $15,000 a *month*—the equivalent of more than $300,000 today.

Just as amazing: How Sarah Rector came into her riches.

It's a story full of ups, downs, and turnarounds, followed by crazy goings-on amid a heap of crimes. But the telling can't begin without a bit of backing up to some facets of American history that are often overlooked.

ONE

160 ACRES

SARAH RECTOR WAS BORN ON MARCH 3, 1902. HER HOME WAS A WEATHER-whipped two-room cabin near the tiny town of Twine, I.T.

I.T. stood for Indian Territory. There, Sarah and her family were known as "Creek freedmen"—that is, black members of a nation of Indians commonly called Creeks.

Mvskoke (mus-KOH-gee) is what these Indians called themselves—Muscogee (and Muskogee) in English. This union of several tribes long included the Euchee, the Tuskegee, and the tribe whose name the union bore, the Muscogee.

As for the men and women, girls and boys, bearing the blood of African tribes, Creeks called them Estelvste (es-stih-LUS-tee)—"the black people."

Some Estelvste lived free among Creeks, making their way as artisans, farmers, and merchants, but most labored in bondage. They were cooks, cleaners, and cowboys. They chopped cotton, plowed cornfields.

While there's no such thing as "good" slavery, there are accounts of some Creek slaveholders treating their captives like kin or "hired hands." Others, however, dealt out body and soul brutalities. They broke up families in sales. They believed in physical abuse, like whippings, sometimes fifty lashes long.

Slaveholding by Creeks didn't begin in I.T. It had gone on in their ancestral homelands in Alabama and Georgia, homelands wrenched from them.

That happened mostly during the 1830s, after years of warfare between white settlers and Indians. Through a combination of bribery and brute force the U.S. government removed almost all members of the Five Tribes of the Southeast (also known as "the Five Civilized Tribes"): the Creek, Cherokee, Chickasaw, Choctaw, and Seminole nations. This was done so that whites could have their rich land. (In parts of north Georgia, that richness included gold.)

ABOVE: "Creek-Negro Type" (1897), artist unknown.

OPPOSITE: A family in the Creek Nation, I.T., c. 1900. Sarah's family lived in a similar cabin.

ECHOHAWK — 1957

"THE FIVE CIVILIZED TRIBES"

The Cherokee, Chickasaw, Choctaw, Creek, and Seminole nations have long been called "the Five Civilized Tribes." White authorities deemed them "civilized" because many of their members embraced some of "the white man's ways." Examples include adopting Euro-American legal codes, farming practices, and dress.

No amount of "civilization" could save these nations from removal when the U.S. government wanted them gone, however. In the 1820s and 1830s, the Five Tribes were pressured into giving up tens of millions of acres in the South: the Cherokees in southeastern Tennessee, northeastern Alabama, and northwestern Georgia; the Chickasaws in northern Mississippi and northwestern Alabama; the Choctaws in central Mississippi and western Alabama; the Seminoles in Florida; and the Creeks in western Georgia and eastern Alabama. These people had already ceded much land decades earlier during the making of early America. ▪

Trail of Tears (1957), inkwash on paper by Brummett Echohawk. The term "trail of years" is most often used to describe the Cherokee journey to Indian Territory, during which some four thousand of them died of hunger, disease, and other causes. The journey to I.T. was also a trail of tears for a multitude of other Indians and for thousands of blacks.

Creek chief Opothle Yoholo (c. 1830) after a painting by Charles Bird King. In 1860, this chief held twenty-five blacks in slavery. The youngest was a one-year-old boy; the oldest, a seventy-five-year-old man. Most members of the Five Tribes were not slaveholders. Within the Creek Nation, for example, in 1860, around 2 percent held about 1,600 blacks in bondage.

And so tens of thousands of adults and children in the Five Tribes were sent west across the mighty river, the Mississippi. They were relocated to the United States' huge unorganized territory—roughly 350 million acres—designated Indian Country in 1834. It bordered Canada on the north and, on the northwest, Oregon Country (held jointly by England and the United States until becoming part of the States in 1846). In the South, Indian Country stopped at Mexico, which then included almost all of today's American Southwest. It stretched from the Mississippi River all the way to the Rocky Mountains in the West. Within Indian Country, millions of acres became known as Indian Territory, or I.T. There, Indians from the Southeast were given new homelands.

Among the more than twenty thousand Creeks forced west of the Mississippi was the Alabama-born chief Opothle Yoholo (o-POTH-le yo-HO-lah). His slaveholdings included Sarah Rector's great-grandma Mollie, who was also born in Alabama. So was her husband, Benjamin, owned by a different Creek man, Reilly Grayson.

The record is silent on Great-Grandma Mollie and Great-Grandpa Benjamin's journey from Alabama, but a snippet of another black couple's experience has survived. It was left to us by their daughter Fannie Rentie Chapman, born in I.T. in the 1850s.

Said Chapman in a 1937 interview: "I remember my parents telling of the movement of the Creeks from Tuskegee, Alabama, to the Indian Territory by steamboat to Fort Gibson in 1836." When another steamboat sank in the mighty river, her parents witnessed the drowning of "many Indians and slaves." Chapman also remembered her family being owned by Wycey Barnwell, a wealthy Creek woman who "cultivated much land."

Chief Opothle Yoholo, Reilly Grayson, Wycey Barnwell, and other Indians who survived the bitter trek west believed that in their new land they would be forever free to rule themselves and keep a river of traditions, such as holding land in common, as a group.

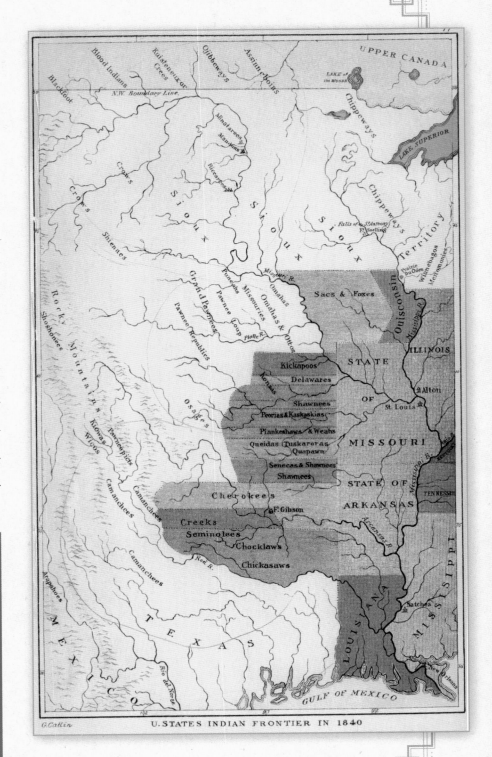

U. STATES INDIAN FRONTIER IN 1840

U. States Indian Frontier in 1840, Shewing [sic] *the Positions of Tribes that have been removed west of the Mississippi* (1841) by George Catlin. As this map shows, the Five Tribes weren't the only Indians removed from the East to the Plains, long home to the Osage, Comanche, and other Indian tribes. By 1840, Indian Country's southern border was no longer Mexico but mostly the Republic (since 1836) of Texas, formed out of the Mexican state Coahuila y Tejas. In 1845, Texas became a U.S. state. Like the states of Louisiana, Arkansas, and Missouri, Indian Country had been part of the 1803 Louisiana Purchase, in which America bought nearly 530 million acres from France, for about $15 million. In 1854, roughly 300 million acres of Indian Country became the organized territories of Kansas and Nebraska.

Those Indians weren't daydreaming about their sovereignty. It had been promised to them in removal treaties. There was also the word of U.S. President Andrew Jackson. In an 1829 message to a group of Creeks, Jackson promised, "Your white brothers will not trouble you; they will have no claim to the land, and you can live upon it, you and all your children, as long as the grass grows or the water runs, in peace and plenty. It will be yours forever."

"Forever" went with the wind for Creeks and other Indians, however. The grass that grew and the water that ran in I.T. lay on ground that over time became a much sought-after commodity by people from the States. Families and single people wanted fresh farmland. Railroad companies wanted to run tracks across the territory. Texas cattle ranchers hankered after pastureland in I.T. and trails through it to get their herds to market. There were also timbermen eyeing I.T.'s forests, and mining outfits craving the coalfields. And some "black gold" (oil) was found. In time, oil companies wagered there was more. So did wildcatters: guys gutsy enough to drill where not a drop of oil had been found for miles.

CREEKS FOR THE UNION

Creek chief Opothle Yoholo was among the Indians in I.T. who opposed siding with the Confederacy. When the Civil War broke out, he declared neutrality. Like-minded Creeks and other Indians gathered at his two-thousand-acre plantation near the Deep Fork River. So did many blacks after the chief sent word promising freedom to all who joined him. He did this in anticipation of attacks by Confederate forces, attacks that came all too soon.

Outgunned and outmanned, Opothle Yoholo's forces eventually fled to Kansas. There, many joined the pro-Union First Indian Home Guard. Among those in Company D was Sarah Rector's grandpa on her mother's side: York McGilbra, who later took the surname Jackson. Grandpa York's regiment saw action in Indian Territory, as well as in Missouri and Arkansas, including the December 1862 Battle of Prairie Grove. This, the bloodiest battle in Arkansas, was a key Union victory. It secured overall Union control of Missouri and north-western Arkansas for the rest of the war.

Sarah's other grandpa, John Rector, served in a different pro-Union regiment: the Second Kansas Colored Volunteer Infantry. ▪

Battle of Round Mountain—November 19, 1861 (1998) by Wayne Cooper. The Battle of Round Mountain (also known as Round Mountains) was the first of several Civil War battles in Indian Territory. Opothle Yoholo's black and Indian warriors faced Confederate forces that included Texas cavalrymen and a Creek battalion under the command of Chilly McIntosh, a prominent member of the tribe and, at the time, a lieutenant colonel in the Confederate army.

The battle flag of the Second Kansas Colored Volunteer Infantry, which fought for the Union mainly in I.T. and Arkansas. Sarah's grandfather John Rector was in Company F (under the alias Jack Benjamin). His regiment was composed of blacks from I.T. and from Arkansas and Missouri, most if not all of whom had escaped slavery. When the Union reorganized black regiments in 1864, Second Kansas became the 83rd USCT (United States Colored Troops). Its brother regiment, the First Kansas Colored Volunteer Infantry, was designated the 79th USCT.

Major change came to Indian Territory after the Civil War (1861–65), in which the Five Tribes had sided with the breakaway southern states, the Confederacy.

Although not all members of the Five Tribes supported the Confederacy, after the Union won the war the tribes as a whole paid a price. In 1866 treaties, the U.S. government demanded that they abolish slavery, which the United States had done through the Thirteenth Amendment to the Constitution in 1865. Even though all blacks who had lived in these Indian nations weren't in slavery before the Civil War, all wound up being called Creek freedmen, Chickasaw freedmen, and so on.

After the war, the Five Tribes were also pressured to make the blacks among them citizens of their nations. Creeks loyal to the Union had already done this, in August 1865. In the April 1866 Civil Rights Act, the U.S. government had granted citizenship to almost all U.S.-born blacks, but not until the Fourteenth Amendment in 1868 was black citizenship (by birth or naturalization) cemented.

Oklahoma Run (1934) by Robert Lindneux. This painting depicts the land run of April 22, 1889. On that day, at high noon, roughly fifty thousand people, who had camped out on I.T.'s borders, raced to claim 160-acre plots in its Unassigned Lands: roughly three million acres ceded by the Creek and Seminole nations after the Civil War. Those who snuck across the border before the starter pistol was fired became known as the "Sooners." "Boomers" were the folks who had lobbied loudly for the Unassigned Lands to be opened up for settlement. The 1889 land run was the first of several. People from the States would also acquire land through lotteries and auctions.

And then there was the land. In the post-war treaties, Indian Territory was reduced to about twenty million acres, as about half of it—the western half—was surrendered to the U.S. government. In 1890, what had been western I.T. became the United States' Oklahoma Territory. There, people from Kansas, Missouri, Texas, and elsewhere got homesteads, largely through "land runs." By 1890, plans were in the works for the takeover of what remained of Indian Territory. The sun was setting on the Indian tradition of holding the land in common. The U.S. government began carving up the land into individual allotments for citizens of Indian nations, making different deals on these allotments with the various nations. With the Creeks, each citizen was due an allotment of up to 160 acres, "more or less."

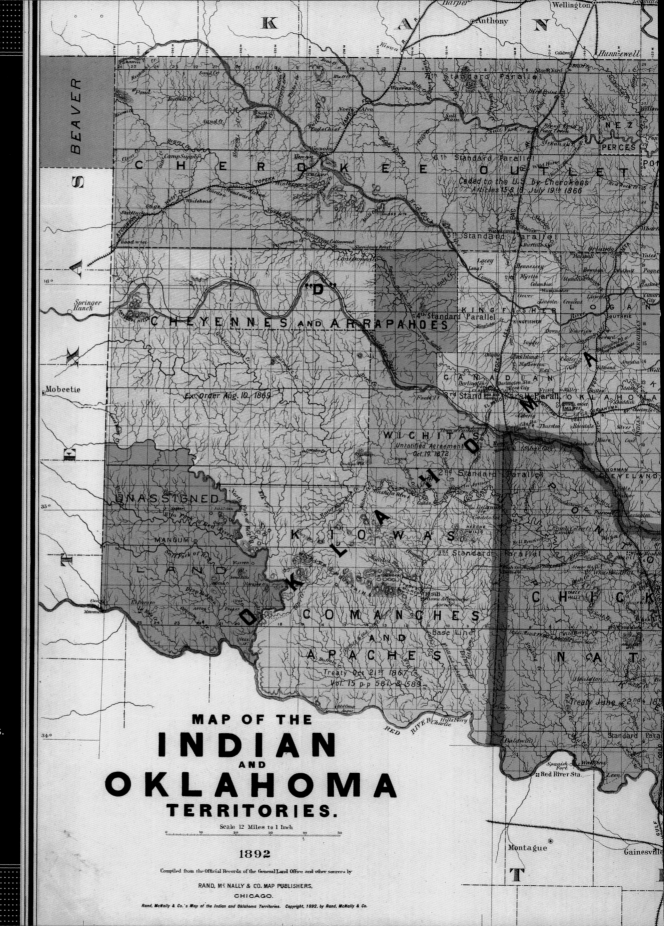

An 1892 map of the "twin territories," I.T. and Oklahoma Territory (but without the entire panhandle). This map shows which land in Oklahoma Territory was still reserved for Indian nations and which land had been settled by people from the States. Ironically, "Oklahoma" comes from the Choctaw *okla* or *ukla* (people) and *humma* or *homma* (red), and so means "land of the red people."

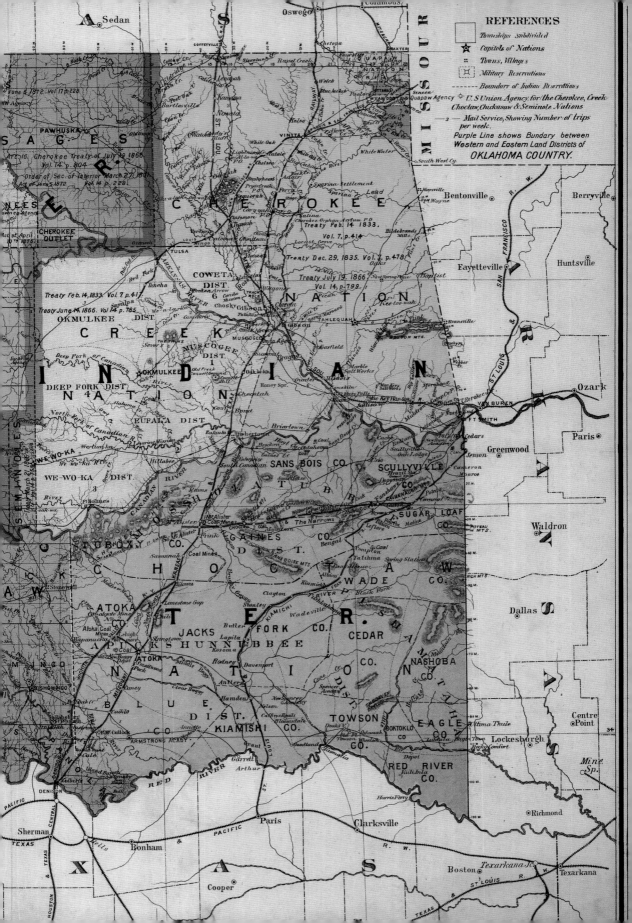

A crowd of Creek freedmen picked allotments about ten miles west of the city of Muskogee, near a place once known as Black Jack. There, they formed the town of Twine.

The breaking up of land into tracts of private property was the beginning of the end of what remained of Indian Territory. On November 16, 1907, Oklahoma Territory and I.T. became one state: Oklahoma.

But what does this have to do with a missing rich black girl?

Where is Sarah Rector?

TWO

THREE AND A HALF DOLLARS AN ACRE

WHEN OKLAHOMA BECAME THE FORTY-SIXTH U.S. STATE IN 1907, SARAH Rector, five years old, was still in her homeplace with her parents, Joe and Rose; her six-year-old sister, Rebecca; her three-year-old brother, Joe Jr.; and her baby sister, Lou Alice.

Twine was no longer the nearest town, however. A new black town, Taft, established a mile or so west in 1904, had taken Twine's place.

A Midland Valley Railroad depot was one of Taft's early points of pride. Others included a soda factory, a grocery store, and a newspaper, the *Enterprise*.

OTHER OKLAHOMA BLACK TOWNS

When Oklahoma became a state in 1907, it had more than two dozen all- or majority-black towns. Along with Taft (Muskogee County), they included Boley (Okfuskee County), Langston (Logan County), and Red Bird (Wagoner County). Another was Bookertee (Okfuskee County), honoring Booker T. Washington, founder of Alabama's Tuskegee Institute and one of the most prominent black men of the day. Some of these towns had been established on land purchased from blacks born in Indian Territory; others, on land acquired in land runs organized by the U.S. government.

Whether populated by "state Negroes" (blacks born outside I.T.), by "natives" (blacks born in I.T.), or by a combination, these towns sprang from a yearning for self-determination and a refuge from racism. By 1920 Oklahoma had about fifty such towns. ▪

The town council of Boley, Oklahoma, c. 1907–10. This Okfuskee County town was established in 1903 on land purchased from a Creek freedman. Boley is one of about a dozen Oklahoma black towns to survive into the twenty-first century. Taft, Langston, and Red Bird are among the others.

Farming was how the Rectors and most folks around Taft made their living, with corn and cotton among the mainstay crops. The land on which Sarah's family farmed and lived lay within her mother's allotment. (Her father had sold part of his and would soon sell the rest.)

Sarah, like her big sister Rebecca and her little brother Joe Jr., had an allotment, too. All three had been born before March 4, 1906, the cutoff date of birth for members of the Creek Nation to get allotments.

Little Lou Alice, born too late for an allotment, didn't miss out on much, it seemed. When Sarah, Rebecca, and Joe Jr. got their acres, the choice land had already been gobbled up. Plus, their allotments weren't even in Muskogee County, where they lived. Rebecca's was down in Okfuskee County. Sarah and Joe Jr.'s land was up in Creek County, about fifty miles northwest of their home.

Sarah's Creek County land wasn't even all in one place. Forty acres were within what once were the boundaries of the township of Mannford. The remaining acres were about eight miles southwest, near a horseshoe bend in the Cimarron River.

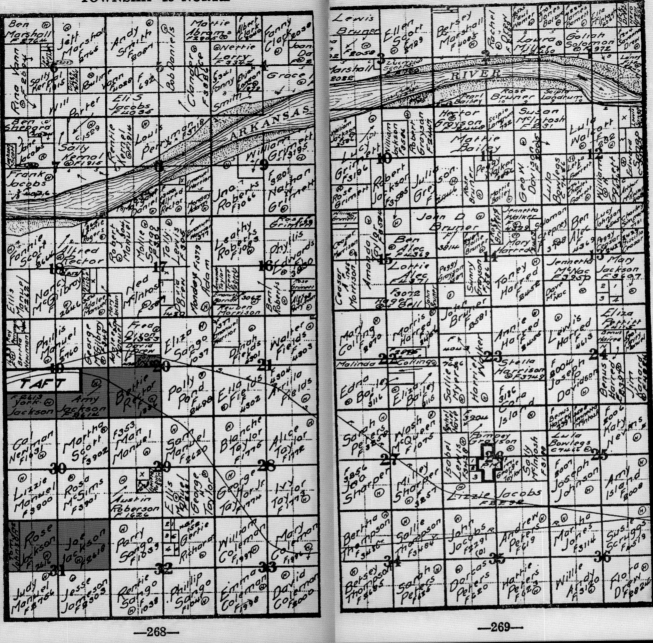

From *Hastain's Township Plats of the Creek Nation* (1910). Seen here are some Creek freedmen allotments around Taft. An "F" before a number stands for "freedman." When Hastain's book was published, of Taft's roughly 350 residents, only about 40 had been born in Oklahoma. Half had been born in Texas.

    The Midland Valley Railroad Company established Taft on acres that once belonged to Sarah's grandparents, Grandpa York and Grandma Amy Jackson. To the right of what is remaining of Amy's allotment is the allotment of Bettie Rector, Sarah's other grandmother. Above Bettie's land is that of her husband, John Rector. It was around his land that Twine had been formed. Sarah's home was on land allotted to her mother, Rose (also known as Rosa) Jackson Rector. Next to her land is that of Joe Jackson, one of her brothers. (The squares with color denote allotments discussed.)

The city of Muskogee, Muskogee County seat, c. 1911.

When assigned to her, Sarah's 160 acres (159.14 acres, to be exact) were valued at a measly $556.50—about three and a half dollars an acre. It was no-account land. Rough. Chock-full of rocks. And a burden besides: Taxes were due, as they were for Rebecca's and Joe Jr.'s land.

The taxes on Sarah's land ran about thirty dollars a year. Not a fortune, but for the Rectors every penny mattered as the family grew. In late 1909, there was another mouth to feed: baby boy Alvin.

Months before Alvin was born, Mr. Rector petitioned the Muskogee County Court to make him the legal guardian of Rebecca, Sarah, and Joe Jr. This would allow him to manage their land, along with any money and personal property they might have, otherwise known as their estates. (Simply being their parent, or natural guardian, didn't automatically qualify him to do all this, legally.)

Mr. Rector's wish was granted on Christmas Eve, 1909. As his children's legal guardian, he could now set about turning their acres from money-drainers into moneymakers.

Not until a year later did Mr. Rector have any success. Working with lawyer O. Benjamin Jefferson, he sold Rebecca's land for $1,700, a good price at the time.

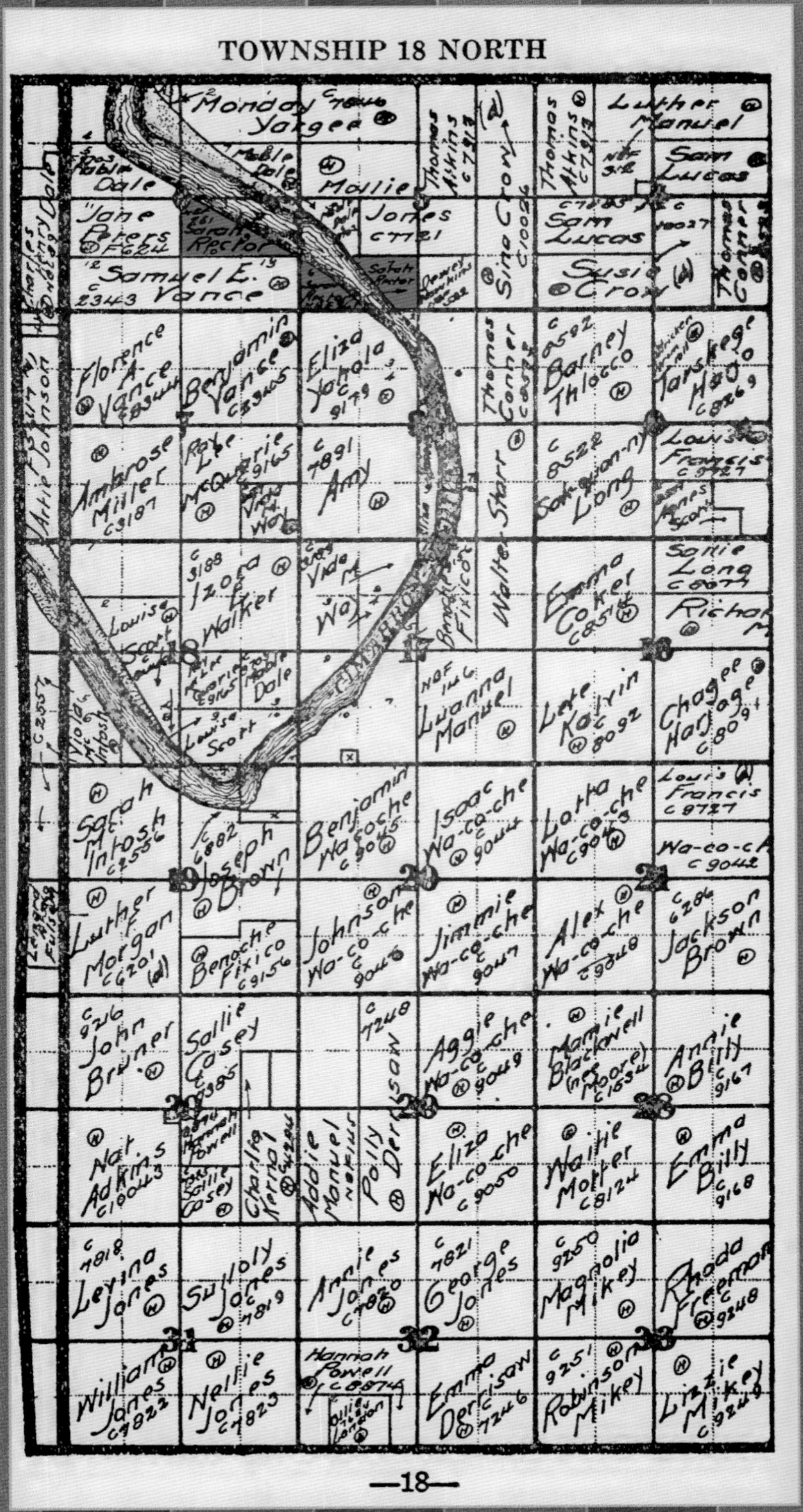

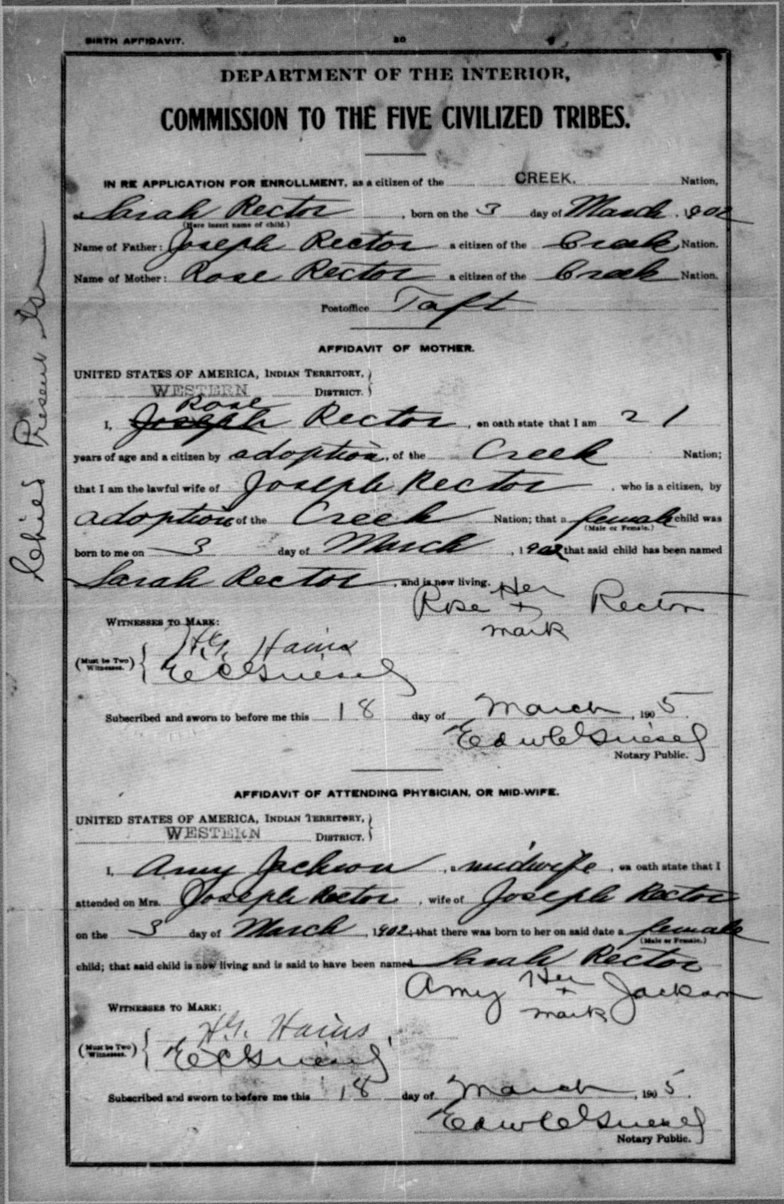

TOWNSHIP 18 NORTH

—18—

DEPARTMENT OF THE INTERIOR,
COMMISSION TO THE FIVE CIVILIZED TRIBES.

19

ABOVE: An important piece of paperwork in the 1905 application for Sarah's allotment. This affidavit (statement of facts under oath) says that Sarah's parents were members of the Creek Nation. Therefore, so was she. The midwife, Amy Jackson, who attested to Sarah's birth on March 3, 1902, was most likely Sarah's maternal grandmother.

LEFT: From *Hastain's Township Plats of the Creek Nation* (1910). Some of Sarah's allotment is seen here: parcels near the horseshoe bend in the Cimarron River (sections 5 and 6, denoted in color).

A bird's-eye view of the Glenn Pool, c. 1910. On November 22, 1905, wildcatters Bob Galbreath and Frank Chesley struck black gold on Ida Glenn's land. Between March 1907 and June 1911, the Glenn Pool produced more than one million barrels of oil per month, except for two months. Because of the Glenn Pool, Tulsa boomed and was known as the "Oil Capital of the World" for many years.

Birds-eye View of Glenn Pool Oil Field near TULSA, Okla.

With Sarah and Joe Jr.'s land, their father wound up seizing opportunities to lease their acreage for oil drilling. And there was a whole lot of that going on, for Oklahoma was in the early days of an oil boom.

So far the biggest pool of oil had been found about twelve miles south of a former nothing of a town, Tulsa. The first strike was on land that belonged to a Creek woman, Ida Glenn, after whom the oil reservoir was named: the Glenn Pool. As the crow flies, the Glenn Pool was about twenty miles southeast of the bulk of Sarah's land.

In February 1911, Mr. Rector leased Sarah's land to Devonian Oil Company in Pittsburgh, Pennsylvania. Upon his signing the contract, Sarah's estate got a bonus of $160, or a dollar an acre. That was all the money that came from that deal, because a year later Devonian scrapped the lease. After that letdown, Sarah's father was ready to wash his hands of her land. On March 18, 1912, he sought the court's okay to sell it. Before he could do that, however, the winds switched again.

In late March, another oil lease deal for Sarah's land came along. This one was with a man named Frank Barnes. But this time, the signing bonus was half as much as in the Devonian deal: only eighty dollars, or fifty cents an acre.

Clearly, word hadn't reached Sarah's father, on the outskirts of Taft, that around daybreak on March 17, wildcatter Tom Slick had struck black gold about five miles south of that horseshoe bend in the Cimarron River. The site of Tom Slick's "Eureka!" was on the land of a white stonemason, Frank Wheeler, and was leased by one of Slick's partners: banker and real estate man B. B. Jones of Bristow, Creek County.

After oil gushed up on Wheeler's land, Tom Slick did his level best to keep his discovery secret—like cutting Wheeler's telephone wire. The wily wildcatter knew that once word got out, a passel of oilmen would make a mad dash to the area to get drilling rights on nearby land.

Thomas Baker Slick (c. 1915). Before he struck oil on Frank Wheeler's land in March 1912, he was mocked as "Dry Hole Slick" and as "Mad Tom Slick." So much of his drilling had been in vain. With the Wheeler strike, Slick's luck switched up. He went on to strike more black gold, including in Texas, and became known as "King of the Wildcatters."

In about a week, Slick and his partners snapped up leases to much of the land several miles around Wheeler's farm. It was B. B. Jones who wound up with the right to drill on Sarah's acres, because within days of getting the lease on her land, Frank Barnes had handed it off to Jones for a dollar. (Barnes was a landman, doing the leasing legwork for Jones.)

To drill on Sarah's land, Jones had to shell out the money for everything his crew had to do, from readying the rig and erecting the derrick to spudding in, then drilling deeper and deeper—hundreds

Cushing-Drumright Field, c. 1912–15. In the car on the left is Bernard Bryan "B. B." Jones, riding shotgun with his brother Robert E. Lee Jones. The white man in the second car is another brother: Montfort. Precisely who the Indians are in both cars is a mystery. Like Sarah, they could be the owners of land Jones leased for oil drilling.

of feet down into the earth. The whole shebang could take one month, two months—maybe more, depending on the technical difficulties the crew ran into.

After all that, if Jones's crew struck very little or no oil—a "dry hole" or a "duster"—he could be out several thousand dollars. But if they struck a "gusher"—oil jetting up fast and furious—B. B. Jones would make big bucks when he sold that crude oil to a refinery, where it would be turned into gasoline, kerosene, and other by-products in high demand.

Sarah would be in the money, too. Her royalty (or share) was the standard 12.5 percent of the oil produced.

Spring 1912 tumbled into summer. Fall floated in, only to be waved away by winter. The Rectors didn't ring in the new year with any glad tidings about Sarah's land. No word of a gusher. Not even of a duster. But by late summer 1913, there was something mighty sweet to celebrate when it came to that land near a horseshoe bend in the Cimarron River.

THREE

TWELVE AND A HALF PERCENT

B. B. JONES'S FIRST WELL ON SARAH'S land was completed on or about August 29, 1913.

It was anything but a duster.

LITTLE SARAH WILL SOON BE IN THE PLUTE CLASS, tooted the *Muskogee Times-Democrat* a few days later. ("Plute" was slang for *plutocrat*, or very wealthy person.)

The paper reported that Sarah's well was producing 2,500 barrels of oil—a whopping 105,000 gallons—a day. With the price of crude oil about a buck a barrel, that was more than $300 a day for Sarah. "Plute" indeed, especially when an ice cream soda cost a nickel.

If that first oil well kept kicking and if B. B. Jones struck other gushers on her land, eleven-year-old Sarah Rector would be able to afford piles of playthings, clothes, and doodads, not to mention a bigger house for her family. It now numbered eight; she had two more sisters: Lillie and Rosa.

Sarah wasn't the boss of her money, however. Until she turned eighteen, she still had to have a guardian.

A gusher in Oklahoma's Cushing-Drumright Field, c. 1912-18.

GUARDIAN ANGEL

In 1908, Kate Barnard, Oklahoma's Commissioner of Charities and Corrections, got riled up over grafter guardians after hearing horror stories. One was of three children living "in the woods near one of our cities," said Barnard at a conference a few years later. She added that she found these children "sleeping in the hollow of an old dead tree, drinking from a nearby stream, and eating at neighboring farmhouses. Their hair was so matted that we had to cut it from their heads." The children's parents were dead.

As for their guardian, he "had been charging exorbitant prices for their schooling and other expenses." When this man was finally tracked down, Barnard discovered another frightening fact: He had fifty-one other wards. Kate Barnard went on to investigate reports of other grafter guardians and to beat the drum for safeguards in the guardianship system. ∎

OKLAHOMA COURTS, BY AND LARGE, had no problem with parents of poor kids being their children's legal guardians, whether black, Indian, white, or whatever. But if a child went from poor to "plute," a court might deem the parent incompetent—unfit to handle the now very valuable estate. In that case, a judge made somebody else the guardian, and it wasn't uncommon for that somebody to be a white man with clout. The same thing even happened to some grown-ups declared incompetent after oil gushed up on their land.

True, some folks needed help with their financial affairs (and certainly young people did), but during Oklahoma's oil boom days, many guardians weren't exactly interested in helping the people whose estates they managed, their wards. Instead, many guardians were into graft: They did low-down, dirty things to get rich at their wards' expense, like billing them for bogus expenses or selling them personal property (often worthless) at sky-high prices. And some guardians did even worse things.

LEFT: Catherine "Kate" Barnard, c. 1910–15. When this Nebraska native became Oklahoma's Commissioner of Charities and Corrections in 1907, she was the first American woman elected to a state post (and at the time, women in America didn't have the national right to vote).

24

In the spring of 1910 the *Muskogee Times-Democrat* ran an article headlined THE STATE IS AFTER GRAFTER GUARDIANS. The authorities were on the hunt for the legal guardians of 143 Indian children with valuable land. These children had been dumped into orphanages while their guardians profited from their estates.

The case of Edith and Edna Durant, Creek freedmen twins with land in the Glenn Pool, had also been in the news. In the summer of 1911, when the girls were going on twelve, banker Bates B. Burnett of Sapulpa had to resign as their guardian. Burnett had failed to account for the twins' money. After months of back-and-forth, he finally agreed to fork over about $40,000.

And Sarah Rector?

As oil gushed up on her acres, Sarah's legal guardian was no longer her father but a white man named T. J. Porter. This farmer and cattle rancher lived in Beland, a few miles south of Taft. Only time would tell if Porter was a saint, a fiend, or something in between.

Meanwhile, the area around Sarah's wells was on its way to eclipsing the great Glenn Pool. Early on, this new oil field was called the Cushing Pool, named for a nearby town. After the town of Drumright sprang up in 1913 around Tom Slick's discovery well, the oil field was sometimes called the Cushing and Drumright oil belt, and eventually the Cushing-Drumright Field.

A FIRE IN THE OIL FIELDS
CUSHING OKLA 8-27.14.   164.

Oil money sometimes went up in smoke. On August 27, 1914, lightning struck the Cushing-Drumright Field, setting off a great fire. Many small oil storage tanks and three 55,000-barrel-capacity tanks were destroyed.

DRUMRIGHT OKLA
THE BUSIEST TOWN IN THE COUNTRY
ELECTRIC STUDIO

The boomtown of Drumright, Oklahoma, c. 1915–18.

Just as in the boomtown of Cushing, many folks in Drumright who supplied drillers, teamsters, and other oil workers with sundry goods, from gear to grub, made money hand over fist.

As Sarah Rector's riches rose, so did the press coverage on her. Sometimes a newspaper just gave a drilling update. The *Muskogee Times-Democrat* did that in late October 1913, reporting that B. B. Jones had brought in more wells on Sarah's land. One was the greatest gusher yet seen in the Cushing-Drumright Field: 4,800 barrels within its first twenty-four hours.

Items on Sarah in other newspapers sometimes served up slapdash facts and fancy. This black girl was a "full-blooded" Indian, some papers said. Others incorrectly reported that she was an orphan, her father having died in prison and her mother from the "white plague" (tuberculosis).

Running through more than a few reports on Sarah Rector's riches was a resentment bordering on rage: vexation over the good fortune of a girl whose forebears had suffered slavery and who herself lived in a state and in a nation where, by law and custom, so many blacks were routinely treated like second-class citizens. Oklahoma's legislature had passed its first Jim Crow law, legalizing segregation in public transportation (trains and trolleys), on December 18, 1907. This was a month after statehood. It was the first bill the lawmakers passed.

In the way that few reports seemed happy for Sarah, not many appeared to give a hoot about her well-being, either. R. S. Abbott's *Chicago Defender*, the leading black-owned newspaper of the day, was one bold exception. RICHEST COLORED GIRL FORCED TO LIVE IN SHACK, raged a front-page headline in November 1913.

Robert Sengstacke Abbott (c. 1919), founder of the *Chicago Defender.*

The article attacked Sarah's guardian. It charged T. J. Porter with getting "a fabulous sum of money a year" but doling out only "a few dollars each month" for Sarah's care. The *Defender* groused about Sarah having a white guardian, insisting that she would be better off with a black one.

The *Defender* beat up on Sarah's parents, too. "Ignorant," it called Joe and Rose Rector—"so ignorant" that they had no idea how much money Sarah's land was making and too ignorant "to insist on a good education and befitting comforts for her."

What thoughts ricocheted around Sarah's head? What feelings were in her heart? How aware was she of the brouhaha over her riches? Did she get wind of the terrible things said about her parents? If she kept a diary, it has disappeared. We are still in search of Sarah's voice.

THOUGH AS A CHILD SARAH HAD NO POWER, NO SAY OVER HER LIFE, AT least on one occasion she rebelled against being the object of curiosity. The *Washington Post* ran an item in late January 1914 that said when a reporter went to Sarah's home, "she refused to come out and see him, but crawled under the bed." This article had a hideous headline: OIL MADE PICKANINNY RICH. The article didn't let up on the insults. It said that Sarah was "ignorant, with apparently little mental capacity."

On the bright side, Sarah would soon have a new home, the piece reported. And there was a lock on her money, it said. No one could legally spend a dollar or a dime of it without the say-so of Muskogee County Court's Judge Thomas Leahy.

Court records bear this out. In late December 1913, T. J. Porter petitioned Judge Leahy for permission to buy twenty acres on which to build Sarah a new home. It would be near the two-room cabin in which she was born, for those twenty acres belonged to Sarah's mother.

For permission to spend Sarah's money on everything that went into the making of her new home, from lumber, screen doors, and fruit trees down to "beds, bedding, chairs, furniture, stoves and various other articles," Porter filed a petition. Judge Leahy said yes to these requests with court orders.

WHILE THAT NEW HOME WAS UNDER CONSTRUCTION AND AFTERWARD, the claptrap and chatter about Sarah Rector's riches kept up. T. J. Porter, said the press, received bushels of letters begging for some of Sarah's cash. Some folks wanted it for charitable endeavors; others for moneymaking schemes.

People wrote to Judge Leahy, too. "I am a poor woman and have a large family and can't work," began a letter from Lydia Doggett in Bay Pond, New York. Having heard that Sarah was getting $15,000 a month, this lady pleaded for one month's income, then told the judge that half the amount would "help a hole lot." Doggett also told Leahy that she knew writing to Sarah would be of "no youse" because it was he who had "the say of the money."

Crazier still, Sarah received marriage proposals—from gold diggers, no doubt: people who claim to love somebody when what they truly love is that person's money. The proposals for Sarah that made the biggest news came from four white men in Germany.

Greed had so many grown-ups behaving so badly.

Even before this mix of madness hit the press, the *Defender* called for Sarah to be taken out of Oklahoma. It wanted her in one of the best schools then available to blacks: Booker T. Washington's Tuskegee Institute, in Tuskegee, Alabama.

"Constant protest and publicity have caused a change for the better," crowed the *Defender* in February 1914. Sarah was in Tuskegee, readers were told. Then, a month later came that alarm-bell article, dated March 14, asking, "Where is Sarah Rector?"

Not in Alabama! Not in Oklahoma!

The paper feared that Sarah's disappearance was "a trick" by T. J. Porter designed to hush the hue and cry for a black guardian. Whatever was afoot, Sarah had to be found, cried Abbott's paper. "Little Sarah Rector can not be hid."

John A. Melby agreed in his letter, urging Abbott to do whatever it took to locate Sarah—even hiring a detective. The *Defender* published Melby's letter under the heading FIND SARAH RECTOR.

In fact, there was reason to worry. Gripped by greed, folks had done worse than swindle or gold-dig people with oil-rich land—they murdered. After the dastardly act, the killer or an accomplice, with forged deeds in hand, laid claim to the dead person's land. Such a scheme had already been at the root of a hellacious crime in Taft.

From the March 14, 1914, *Chicago Defender*.

RICHEST CHILD OF THE RACE MYSTERIOUSLY DISAPPEARS

Little Sarah Rector Is Not In Oklahoma and Is Not the Child of That Name Under the Care of Dr. Booker T. Washington at Tuskegee Institute.

WHITE GUARDIAN CARELESS.

Evidently Lured Away by Candy and a Handful of Pennies—When at Home She Lived in Hut and Had No Playthings Like Other Children.

Where is Sarah Rector?

That is a question that everyone from Oklahoma to Tuskegee, Ala., is trying to answer. Little Sarah Rector, the 10 year old girl, is not at her home near the Creek river in Oklahoma, nor is she under the care of Principal Booker T. Washington at Tuskegee Institute. Under date of February 14 The Chicago Defender published a story telling of her vast possessions, and stating that she was then at Tuskegee Institute.

Another Sarah Rector.

This week Mr. Emmett J. Scott, secretary to Hon. Booker T. Washington, in a letter to this newspaper states that "the Sarah Rector at Tuskegee is not the girl of Muskogee." Inquiry in and around Muskogee enlists the fact that she is not there, and the question again arises:

Where is Sarah Rector?

Trick of White Guardian.

The Chicago Defender and other newspapers have recently engaged in a campaign to have this child taken out of the hands of her white guardian and put in the care of a member of her own race so that she could be educated and fitted in every way to handle her vast wealth when she becomes of age, and it is feared that her disappearance is a trick to offset such a move on the part of her white guardian.

Sarah Rector Must Be Found.

Little Sarah Rector can not be hid. She is of too much importance to the members of her race, who intend to have her live in the open like respectable people should. Her guardian realizes a princely sum in the handling of her fortune, and it is as little as he can do to send her to school and take her out of the hovel that she has previously called home. Careful search is being made for her. Meanwhile nature in the shape of fine oil wells daily piles up dollars for her, but the all important question now is:

Where is Sarah Rector?

LEFT: Tuskegee Institute founder Booker Taliaferro Washington, c. 1905. In November of that year, Washington made one of his visits to Muskogee. There he delivered a speech on a platform erected on the corner of Okmulgee and Second Street. Thousands of people in a crowd "composed of black, white and red were held spell-bound from beginning to end," reported the *Muskogee Cimeter*. Among the things Washington said: "Here in the South both races labor under a disadvantage, because the bad that there is among whites and blacks is, almost without exception, flashed all over the country, while the worthy acts of both races are seldom known beyond the borders of the community or state."

RIGHT: A bird's-eye view of Tuskegee Normal and Industrial Institute, in Tuskegee, Alabama, c. 1907. The school earned high marks for its teacher training and vocational education (from carpentry and shoemaking to farming).

The victims were two Creek freedmen, a brother and sister, whom Sarah may have known: twelve-year-old Herbert and ten-year-old Stella Sells. His allotment was in Muskogee County, near Haskell; hers was in the Glenn Pool. Both these children died in the early morning hours of March 23, 1911, when their house exploded. It was soon discovered that dynamite had been packed beneath their bedroom!

Several white men (one a former Muskogee city councilman) and several black men were arrested for the crime. The children's stepfather, Zebidee Mackey, was one of them, but the case against him was dismissed. (Their mother, Priscilla, was never suspected of any involvement.)

In the end, two men, one black, one white, were sentenced to life in the state penitentiary for the murders of Herbert and Stella Sells.

Taft Dynamiting Case Is Called

REVISED THE CONTRACT

The preliminary skirmish of what is to be the most important murder case ever tried in Oklahoma, was begun before Judge R. P. deGraffenreid today when Owen and Stone, attorneys for Doc Allen, a negro charged with being one of the men who dynamited the Zeb Mackey home at Taft March 22, made a motion to have the case against Allen dismissed on the grounds that Allen was not tried at the term of court following his indictment. The Mackey home was blown up by dynamite and Estella and Herbert Sells, aged 12 and 14, children of Mrs. Mackey by her first husband, blown up and burned to death. Allen was arrested a few days later and his attorneys contend he should have been tried in the May term of court.

The motion was overruled.

Irwin Case Delayed.

Will Irwin, a white man and prominent real estate dealer, who was arrested in the city of Mexico with a deed to the land of one of the Sells children, was to be placed on trial this morning, but the motion to dismiss the case against Al-

In order to satisfy County Commission W. T. Cole, and straighten out a clause in the contract relative to the finishing of the interior that seemed ambiguous, the contract of the county commissioners with T. H. Martin for the leasing of the five top stories on an eight-story court house building to be erected on Second and Court streets, was today revised by Mr. Martin and the commissioners.

This makes the objectionable clause very clear and states specifically that T. H. Martin is to build all the walls in the part of the building leased, is to plaster the same, etc.

This is said to be highly satisfactory toward all concerned. Commissioner Cole did not sign the contract the other day, but with these objections removed he will probably affix his signature with the other commissioners this afternoon.

From the December 11, 1911, *Muskogee Times-Democrat*. The men sentenced to life in prison for killing Herbert and Stella Sells were William "Bill" Irvin, a white landman, and a black man named D. R. "Doc" Allen, a blacksmith. Irvin died in prison in 1916. Allen, who had pled guilty under questionable circumstances, was paroled in 1918 and received a full pardon in 1926. The authorities evidently believed Allen's claim that, while he had been asked to plant the dynamite, he had refused for fear of blowing his head off. He had offered to kidnap the children and take them to Mexico instead.

So where was Sarah Rector when the *Defender* was in a frenzy, fearing her kidnapped?

Hidden away by T. J. Porter?

Nope.

Wooed away by a gold-digging German or other money-grubbing man?

Not at all.

Murdered?

Thank goodness, no.

The *Defender* had been woefully wrong. In April 1914, it reported that she was in Oklahoma after all.

RIGHT: William Edward Burghardt Du Bois (standing center) in the offices of the *Crisis* in Lower Manhattan, New York City, date unknown.

OPPOSITE: Men at work on an oil storage tank in Oklahoma's Cushing-Drumright Field, c. 1912–18.

THE *DEFENDER* STILL DIDN'T REST EASY. IT CONTINUED TO CONTEND that Sarah wasn't being treated right. The National Association for the Advancement of Colored People (NAACP) feared the same thing. This New York City–based civil rights organization had reported on Sarah in its magazine, the *Crisis*.

In the spring of 1914, attorney James C. Waters Jr., an NAACP special agent, wrote to several officials, including Oklahoma's governor, Lee Cruce. In his reply, the governor informed Waters that in his view Sarah's estate "has been exceptionally well managed." Cruce also told Waters, in so many words, to mind his own business.

In contrast, Muskogee County's Judge Thomas Leahy was quite gracious when he answered a letter from the renowned scholar-activist W. E. B. Du Bois, an NAACP founder and editor of the *Crisis*. In acknowledging receipt of Du Bois's June 6 letter seeking "the facts," Leahy mentioned Du Bois's promise to keep his reply "in strictest confidence." No need for that, Leahy told him. "[Y]ou may use this letter for any purpose that you see fit, as I have no desire for it to be treated confidential."

The judge then got down to "the facts."

FOUR

ONE MILLION DOLLARS

SARAH'S INCOME?

She was "plute," all right, but as Judge Leahy revealed to Du Bois, contrary to rumor, Sarah wasn't getting $15,000 a month from her oil wells.

Her first money came in October 1913: $11,567.29. The next month, Sarah received $6,130.15. The amount continued to vary. In May 1914, for example, it was $1,171.51. All told, Sarah had gotten $54,490.22 in oil revenue.

What about her home?

Sarah and her family lived in a five-room cottage. With "a well, outbuildings and other improvements," her new home cost about $1,700, wrote Leahy. The judge even went into detail on the purchase

Halochee Industrial Institute in Taft, date unknown. Seen here, before one of the school's buildings, is its "model department," that is, its elementary school. Another of Taft's schools was the W. T. Vernon School, likely the one Sarah and her siblings attended.

of those twenty acres from Mrs. Rector, explaining that he had been behind the idea, as it helped the family on two counts.

Leahy wanted Sarah to own her home, free and clear—including the ground beneath it. That way if her parents fell into financial trouble, no one could boot Sarah off the land. (At the time, Mrs. Rector was in dangerous debt. She had borrowed a great deal of money against her land, which was about to be foreclosed upon. Sarah's estate came to her rescue by buying those twenty acres for $900, then making her a loan.)

Next, Judge Leahy dealt with Sarah's schooling. She and two siblings (presumably, Rebecca and Joe Jr.) went to a school in Taft, "two miles distant." The kids used to walk there until the judge learned in conversation with Mr. Rector that one of his horses was "too old to work." But as this horse was "perfectly gentle and safe for these children to drive," Leahy told Mr. Rector that if he supplied the horse, Sarah's estate would buy a buggy and a harness.

But why wasn't Sarah in a top school available to blacks? Early on, Leahy explained, he had urged Sarah's parents to send her to just such a school right away, but they balked at the idea, thinking Sarah too young. Mr. and Mrs. Rector had, however, agreed to let her go away to school in the coming fall.

Evidently, Du Bois also had asked for confirmation that Sarah's guardian was white, for at one point the judge wrote: "As to this ward having a white guardian, this is true." Leahy then added something that surely shocked Du Bois: "The parents themselves selected him."

T. J. Porter, said the judge, had been the family's "benefactor for years and long before there was any probability of their ever having any money."

We'll probably never know if Du Bois frowned, scratched his head, or fell out of his chair when he read that.

The parents themselves selected him?

Indeed. And had the NAACP, the *Defender*, or anybody else worried about Sarah Rector heeded Mr. Melby's advice and hired a detective to "get at the facts" down in Muskogee County, that detective likely would have dropped by the courthouse.

If this sleuth got hold of court records, he or she would have discovered that in July 1913—before Sarah's first gusher—Mr. Rector resigned as legal guardian. He and his wife then asked the court to let Porter take his place.

As for the "fabulous sum of money a year" the *Defender* claimed Porter was getting: $900 so far. That was less than 2 percent of Sarah's income, Leahy pointed out. (A guardian fee of 2 to 6 percent was commonplace.)

Porter's work included making Sarah's money make money, mostly through first-mortgage loans. That meant borrowers put up, as collateral, real estate they owned (as Sarah's mother had done). If they didn't pay Sarah back, she had first dibs on their property. Leahy told Du Bois that so far Porter had lent out more than $40,000 belonging to Sarah, at 8 percent interest. (Local banks paid 4 percent interest on deposits at that time.)

And the money for Sarah's day-to-day care—what the *Defender* called "a few dollars" a month? What about that?

In November 1913, Sarah's father began getting fifty of Sarah's dollars a month. Then in May 1914, Leahy signed off on upping that to $65, the equivalent of about $1,500 today. Not exactly chump change, given that the family lived in Sarah's house and her estate paid for outfitting and maintaining it.

Judge Leahy said he'd increase the allowance if he thought it would do Sarah some good, which he didn't. "I do not believe that her money should be spent and other members of the family and neighbors get the benefits just because she has it."

And this "she" was one very lucky little girl on several counts. Not only did Sarah wind up with oil-rich land, but her guardian wasn't a grafter. What's more, she had a judge looking out for her.

Could Leahy have fed Du Bois a pack of lies? Anything's possible. But how foolhardy to lie, in writing, to somebody with a national magazine—and on top of that tell him there's no need to keep mum about the letter. Besides, Leahy didn't have a reputation as a liar. Or as a fool. Or as a corrupt judge.

When Leahy answered Du Bois, he was seeking reelection (which he won). During the campaign, the *Haskell News* hailed the judge as "honest." It also called him "a terror" to bad guardians.

It was Leahy who had gone after banker Bates B. Burnett, guardian of the twins Edith and Edna Durant. (Like Sarah, they lived in Muskogee County, and so their estates were under Leahy's jurisdiction, but Leahy wasn't the judge who had appointed Burnett their guardian.)

Around the time that Leahy dealt with Burnett, he got a thumbs-up on a different matter from a weekly billed as "the oldest colored paper in Oklahoma": W. H. Twine's *Muskogee Cimeter*. "It takes an awful big man to give the Negro a square deal and Muskogee's judge is such a man," cheered the *Cimeter*.

As for the charge that Sarah's parents were too "ignorant" to demand "befitting comforts" for her, Leahy's letter didn't say anything about this. But given that Sarah had no oil money until October 1913, it's not scandalous that a new house wasn't on the drawing board until December. Why not a larger, more luxurious house? Were Sarah and her family being treated shabbily? Or was caution the best course early on?

William Henry Twine (c. 1902). His building on Muskogee's South Second Street housed his newspaper, his law office, and other businesses. Twine was known as the "Black Tiger" because he was such a fierce crusader for racial justice. Born in Kentucky, Twine also lived in Ohio, Indiana, then Texas. He moved to Indian Territory in 1891. The town of Twine was named for him.

ABOVE: Inside Muskogee's First National Bank on Broadway and Main, c. 1910. Sarah had an account at this bank.

OPPOSITE: An October 1917 ad for the car that the court allowed Sarah's estate to buy in the summer of 1917 for $2,096. The woman in the ad, Trixie Friganza, was a vaudeville star.

What if Sarah's oil wells went dry after a short while?

What if the price of crude oil dropped?

With such unknowns, what was more important: for Sarah to have a big house and a lavish lifestyle, or for her to have money in the bank (and money making more money on deposit at banks and through lending)?

And it seems that Sarah did have "comforts." Back in February 1914, Judge Leahy had allowed Porter to spend about thirty bucks on a phonograph for her. That May, the purchase of a piano had been okayed. In time, rooms were added to Sarah's home. So was a garage for a snappy Premier motorcar (later chucked for a seven-passenger Cadillac).

Yes It's a *Premier*

TRIXIE FRIGANZA SAYS:
"What a beauty, and a cinch to drive."

Call us up and let us prove to you what a wonderful car this is

WM. T. PATTEN MOTOR CO. Phone East 251
1409 12th Ave.

JUDGE LEAHY ON THE WARPATH

As the following snippets from newspaper accounts reveal, wrongdoing and greed knew no color. These excerpts are from white-owned newspapers. Typically, unless someone was black, his or her race wasn't mentioned.

Since the first of the year County Judge Thos. Leahy has removed fifteen guardians for irregularities. . . .

"Grafting has got to stop in Muskogee County and Indian minors will be protected so long as I have anything to say about it," the judge is credited with saying.

—"JUDGE LEAHY GOES AFTER GUARDIANS," *MUSKOGEE TIMES-DEMOCRAT*, MAY 9, 1911

Lewis T. Brown, a negro attorney, was fined five dollars by . . . Judge Leahy today for failing to file a report of guardian in the case of Ralph Mason, a minor.

—"ATTORNEY FINED," *MUSKOGEE TIMES-DEMOCRAT*, JUNE 24, 1911

Clay Brown of Pryor Creek, guardian of Rilla and Freedman Bruner, was arrested yesterday . . . after [Leahy] discovered a discrepancy in the guardian's accounts. . . .

Warner Bruner, father of the children, an ignorant negro about 60 years old, was arrested for complicity.

—*MUSKOGEE TIMES-DEMOCRAT*, JULY 15, 1911

Walter [Doherty], a [mixed-blood Cherokee], who was found to be over seven thousand dollars short in his account in the affairs of his three minor children for whom he was guardian, resigned. . . .

Judge Leahy granted [him] two weeks time to pay the amount over to the new guardian with six per cent interest.

—"DR. THOMPSON IS GUARDIAN," *MUSKOGEE TIMES-DEMOCRAT*, APRIL 25, 1912

[Hosea] A. Langford was the guardian of two negro minors and was charged by County Judge Leahy with embezzlement of $2,500 from the estate of the minors last year. Langford skipped out and went down into Texas. His bondsmen, however, made good the shortage and Judge Leahy did not continue the search for him.

—"APPEARANCE BOND FOR LANGFORD," *MUSKOGEE TIMES-DEMOCRAT*, JUNE 15, 1914

JUDGE THOS. W. LEAHY.

Candidate to Succeed Himself for Judge of the County Court.

Mineral Point, Wisconsin–born Judge Thomas William Leahy in the July 30, 1914, *Haskell News*. It was on June 11, 1914—the date of Leahy's letter to W. E. B. Du Bois—that Oklahoma's Supreme Court issued eighteen rules for guardians (effective July 15, 1914). Some rules were par for the course in Judge Leahy's court, such as not spending a ward's money without a court order. Other rules pertained to extra oversight. For example, for Sarah and other members of the Creek Nation, the Creek National Attorney and the U.S. government's probate attorney (one who specialized in estates) could monitor their affairs.

A festive day, in the early 1900s, at the Children's House at Tuskegee Institute, now Tuskegee University. According to the university, Sarah and Rebecca were enrolled at the Children's House from December 12, 1914, to September 7, 1915, and "Mr. T. J. Porter was their responsible party/guardian at the time of their attendance."

Before Sarah's house was enlarged, before cars were purchased, before somebody ran up bills for hundreds of dollars at Chandler's, a Muskogee department store (one for dresses, shoes, hats, fabric, perfume, a parasol, and more), and before an okay to spend forty-five bucks on a gold watch for Sarah—before all this, in the fall of 1914, twelve-year-old Sarah Rector and her thirteen-year-old sister, Rebecca, were being readied for a trip to the Southeast. They were going to Alabama, where their great-grandparents Mollie and Benjamin had been born. The girls' final destination was Tuskegee Institute's elementary school, the Children's House.

By the time Sarah went to Tuskegee in 1914, B. B. Jones had drilled many more wells on her allotment. Come summer 1918, there were fifty. Only one had been abandoned. Prairie Oil and Gas, a Kansas-based outfit, had the lease by then, having paid a $300,000 signing bonus!

Over the years, a boatload of Sarah's bucks—more than a quarter-million—was invested in real estate. Most of this money bought farmland, which was then rented out. In the adjoining counties of Muskogee and Wagoner, for example, Sarah owned more than two thousand acres of prized river bottom land.

In the city of Muskogee, Sarah owned a two-story building on South Second Street. Upstairs was a forty-odd-room boardinghouse; downstairs were several stores, including a bakery and the Busy Bee Café. The man running this café, Harry Kourtis, soon took over the lease on the boardinghouse and turned it into the Busy Bee Hotel.

BELOW: Busy, buzzing Kansas City, Missouri, c. 1917.

SECOND STREET, MUSKOGEE, OKLA.

HAND-COLORED

ABOVE: Muskogee's Second Street in the early 1900s, looking south. Sarah's building, purchased for $57,000 in 1915, was at 213–223 South Second Street, across the street from the Convention Hall and a few hundred feet from two train stations.

131. MAIN STREET BY NIGHT, KANSAS CITY, MO.

On top of revenue from oil, moneylending, and rental property, Sarah had other sources of income: interest from U.S. savings bonds, for example. And it all added up. When Sarah turned eighteen, on March 3, 1920, she was worth an estimated $1 million (about $11 million today).

Where was this truly "plute" young lady then?

Sarah Rector wasn't living near Taft, nor in Tuskegee. She was in Kansas City, Missouri, where her family had relocated a few years earlier. There, the Rectors eventually moved into a home that was a far cry from that weather-whipped two-room cabin in which Sarah began life. This homeplace was a stately stone house. It became known as the Rector Mansion.

$51,414

Before Sarah's guardian could buy property for her, there had to be a hearing. On November 3, 1916, there was a hearing concerning roughly five hundred acres in Muskogee and Wagoner Counties.

In attendance were Sarah's father; T. J. Porter; Porter's attorney, Edward Curd Jr.; and W. M. Harrison, U.S. probate attorney representing the Creek Nation. Also present was the man taking the lead in selling the land, Walter Scott.

Judge Glenn Alcorn was presiding. Months earlier, Judge Leahy had decided to enter private law practice.

JOE RECTOR, being first duly sworn,
   on oath testifies as follows:

BY MR. CURD [Porter's attorney]:

Q State your name.

A Joe Rector. . . .

Q You know about the proposed purchase of land through this court by Mr. Porter?

A Yes, sir. . . .

Q You have made an investigation of this land yourself?

A Yes, sir. . . .

BY THE COURT [Judge Alcorn]:

Q Joe, how old is Sarah at this time?

A Fourteen and past.

Q She lives with you and her mother?

A Yes, sir.

Q You live out near Boynton?

A Near Taft. . . .

Q Are you a member of the Creek tribe of Indians?

A Yes, sir, freedman. . . .

Q Do you believe that the investment of $51,414 in this land would be a good investment for your minor child?

A Yes, sir, I do. . . .

Q How many times have you been on that land?

A Three. . . .

Q Is this what is known as Arkansas River land?

A It is Grand River bottom land. . . .
   Witness dismissed.

T. J. PORTER, being first duly sworn,
   on oath testifies as follows:

BY MR. CURD:

Q Your name is T. J. Porter?

A Yes, sir.

Q You are the guardian of Sarah Rector?

A Yes, sir.

Q Mr. Porter, you filed petition to purchase 514.14 acres of land in Grand River bottoms, across from Fort Gibson. Have you investigated that land yourself?

This postcard (c. 1916) shows some of Sarah's oil-rich allotment, also known as her "farm."

Sarah Rector farm on the Cimarron.

A Yes, sir.

Q Been over it?

A Two times.

Q Did Joe Rector, the father of this ward, go with you?

A Yes, sir, he went once. . . .

BY THE COURT:

Q You say that you have been on this land several times?

A No, just twice. . . .

Q You have about how much cash on hand belonging to this minor?

A About $130,000.

Q In cash?

A Yes, sir.

Q What is the average income, monthly, of this minor?

A About $800 a month. I mean $8,000.

Q And that money is derived from her oil royalties?

A Yes, and interest. . . .

Q About how much money loaned out? . . .

A $60,000. . . .

Q Is there any likelihood that [Sarah's] income from the oil production will materially decrease in the next few months?

A Went off some last month, but they might not have been pumping it regularly, can't tell, it is holding up good. . . .
Witness dismissed. . . .

WALTER SCOTT, being first duly sworn, on oath testifies as follows:

BY MR. CURD:

Q Your name is Walter Scott?

A Yes, sir.

Q Are you a citizen of the Cherokee Nation?

A Yes, sir. . . .

Q Most of the land proposed to be sold to Sarah Rector, through the court, belongs to you and your family?

A Yes, sir, and I bought a freedman's.

The hearing continued the next day, and in December the court approved the purchase.

EPILOGUE

SARAH RECTOR'S ROAD TO TAKING CONTROL OF HER RICHES WAS ROUGH and rocky, just like her allotment. Before she turned eighteen, eventually there was drama.

By law, at age fourteen Sarah could have her say about whom she wanted as guardian. In October 1916, she nominated T. J. Porter and her father. Muskogee County's Judge Glenn Alcorn, Leahy's successor, presided over the hearing on the proposed Porter-Rector guardianship. When asked if he felt fit to manage his daughter's estate, Mr. Rector replied, "Yes, sir." Sarah's father believed that things would be just fine with him and T. J. Porter assisting each other. He also remarked that Porter had always seemed "fair and square, and I never have heard of him dealing with anybody any other way."

Later, after Judge Alcorn hinted that he was going to appoint "some businessman" as Porter's co-guardian instead of Mr. Rector, Sarah and her parents nominated a white man named Milton G. Young to be that person. Young was an officer at Muskogee's Exchange National Bank, one of the banks where Sarah had an account.

The Porter-Young guardianship didn't last long. In August 1917, Porter resigned—"under fire," reported the *Muskogee Times-Democrat*. That "fire" came from R. C. Allen, the Creek National Attorney. He charged Porter and his lawyer, Edward Curd Jr., with enriching themselves at Sarah's expense.

Porter wasn't found guilty of any wrongdoing, but his attorney was. Over the course of four years Curd had taken nearly $8,500 in "secret commissions"—kickbacks—on some investments, mostly real estate. During that time, Sarah's estate had paid him about $6,800 for his services. Curd lost his law license. He also was sued by Sarah's new joint guardians: Milton G. Young and another white man, Charles A. Looney, managing editor of the *Muskogee Times-Democrat*.

Curd was one of several lawyers—some white, some black—caught up in a probe. Among the black lawyers was O. Benjamin Jefferson, almost certainly the same man Mr. Rector had helping him when he was Sarah's guardian. Charged with misconduct in the affairs of his former ward, Jefferson had his law license suspended for six months. His former ward, Stella (Manuel) Mason, was another oil-rich Creek freedman.

....

CURD'S DOUBLE-DEALING WASN'T THE END OF THE DRAMA. AROUND THE time that Sarah turned eighteen in 1920—and for a couple of years after—people (related to her and not) sought control of her estate. The underlying claim was that she was unfit to handle her financial affairs. Finally, in 1922 Sarah was free of legal challenges over being boss of her riches. She was twenty years old—an adult, not a child who needed guardianship.

Sarah was still living in Kansas City when that day came. There, she spent her money as she pleased. It pleased her to buy real estate and to make other investments. It also pleased her to splurge on expensive cars, clothing, jewels, furs, and other fancies that fit the high life. She was definitely in step with the times. Sweeps of folks were living like money grew on trees.

More and more skyscrapers were going up in big, broad cities. The stock market was soaring. Up, too, was the number of nightclubs and dance halls, for this was the Jazz Age. And Kansas City, Missouri, was a capital city of this new, hot music.

George E. Lee's Kansas City–based band.

Chances are Sarah shared her riches with Kenneth Campbell, whom she married in September 1922, when she was twenty and he was nineteen.

Sarah didn't spend all her days living the high life. She was soon the mother of three boys: Kenneth Jr., Leonard, and Clarence, the last one born in August 1929. Her marriage, however, didn't last. By April 1930, Kenneth Sr. was in Chicago, where he became a city councilmember years later.

As for Sarah, by April 1930, home was no

longer the Rector Mansion but a modest house at 2440 Brooklyn Avenue. Living with her and her sons were her sister Rebecca (who worked as a housekeeper) and their mother's mother, Amy.

Sarah's mother, Rose, lived not far away on Wabash Avenue with the rest of her children. Joe Jr., who was now twenty-four, was a truck driver; Lou Alice, twenty-one, worked in a hat shop; Alvin, twenty, was a chauffeur; and Lillie, eighteen, who would die of tuberculosis before year's end, was still in school. Presumably, so were the rest of Sarah's siblings: Rosa, sixteen; Arthur, fourteen (born in Oklahoma); and Roy, eleven (born in Missouri). Sarah's father had died in July 1922, a few months before she married Kenneth.

Sarah married again, in 1934, to William Crawford, who owned a restaurant. And with him she lived the rest of her days.

ABOVE: The Rector Mansion at 2000 East 12th Street (at Euclid) in Kansas City, Missouri.

OPPOSITE, BOTTOM: Sarah Rector and Kenneth Campbell, c. 1922. Kansas-born Kenneth Campbell had several businesses in Kansas City, Missouri. One was a car dealership, located in the heart of the city's black downtown, in the famous 18th and Vine district, the cradle of Kansas City jazz. (This image has been reproduced from a deteriorating newspaper page, which accounts for its poor quality. The image above is from the same source.)

Sarah Rector Campbell Crawford died on July 22, 1967, following a stroke. A few days later, she was buried a few miles from her first homeplace, in Taft's Blackjack Cemetery.

Was she "plute" when she passed? No, but neither was Sarah a pauper. She still had some property in Missouri, for example. As for her real estate in Oklahoma, most, if not all, of it was gone through sale or foreclosure by 1933. Gone, too, by then was her allotment. Sarah sold those acres in November 1932 to a Herman Epstein for $100 and "other valuable considerations." At the time, more than a dozen of her wells had been abandoned, and others would be in years to come. But not all. There were wells in operation into the twenty-first century.

Dick's Down Home Cook Shop at 1521 East 18th Street, c. 1929. The restaurant owned by Sarah's second husband was at 1518 East 18th Street.

OVER THE YEARS FOLKS HAVE SPECULATED ABOUT WHAT HAPPENED TO Sarah Rector's riches.

Did she live too lavishly?

Was she mooched on by dodgy "friends"?

It could be that during the Roaring Twenties, Sarah, like thousands of other people, bought over-hyped stocks and made other bad investments, then suffered big losses in the 1929 stock market crash, tripwire for the Great Depression.

The search continues for more information on the person once ballyhooed as the richest black girl in America. No easy task. As an adult, she no longer hid under the bed to escape unwanted attention, but, as her son Clarence told a reporter in the 1990s, Sarah Rector was "a very private person."

AUTHOR'S NOTE

IN JUNE 2010, SHERELLE HARRIS, ASSISTANT DIRECTOR OF THE NORWALK Public Library System in Norwalk, Connecticut, alerted me to a 2009 online post by historian Stacey Patton: "Sarah Rector: The Richest Colored Girl in the World."

Sarah Rector was news to me. In search of more information, I soon found Patton's longer piece about her in the spring 2010 issue of the *Crisis* magazine. Intrigued, I went in further search of Sarah Rector: in countless newspaper and magazine articles from the early 1900s, in forty, maybe fifty, pounds of documents from the National Archives, Muskogee County District Court, and other institutions.

Sadly, I never found an account of Sarah's life in her own words, but I kept on with the research, with the writing, because I found the story of her lucky allotment so fascinating—and quite a window onto aspects of American history that aren't much talked about. I also found object lessons in Sarah's story.

Sarah Rector's riches give people of all ages food for thought on handling money, whether windfall or wages. How to spend? How to save? How to invest?

Sarah's story also reminds us to use discernment when reading those "first drafts" of history. So often, the farther the offices of periodicals (both black and white) were from Oklahoma, the more distorted and bizarre the picture they painted of what was going on in Sarah's life. Not surprising. Back then, there were no jet planes, no high-speed trains, no interstate highways. Long-distance travel for most reporters, like everybody else, was no easy feat. Also, telephones weren't abundant, and many people did not even have them in their homes. When it came to nonlocal news, many periodicals filled pages with cut-and-pastes from other news outlets.

In doing my best to sort out facts from fictions and confusions about Sarah's life, I also searched for her longest-serving legal guardian, T. J. Porter. At the outset I expected to find evidence that he was a fiend, because for decades the word was that during Oklahoma's oil boom days *all* white guardians of people with valuable land were grafters. There was also the claim that no blacks were allowed to be guardians of wealthy children. Finding neither to be true—well, there's another lesson: Better to rest on research and reason than on scuttlebutt.

....

IN A 1916 COURT HEARING, SARAH'S FATHER STATED THAT WHEN HE AND his wife chose Porter to be guardian, he had known the man for seven or eight years. Details on their relationship remain a mystery.

So was T. J. Porter. Early on I didn't discover much about the man, but in newspaper articles, I found a T. J. Porter linked to an E. T. Werhan. In 1907, for elections in the Beland area, when an E. T. Werhan was running for justice of the peace, a T. J. Porter was running for constable. A few years later, when a T. J. Porter was a member of the Beland School Board, an E. T. Werhan was clerk of the board. The newspaper item on this said that the two men co-owned three hundred acres of land.

Among the court documents I acquired was the guardianship bond Porter had provided the court, a document I initially gave only a glance. When I finally gave it a hard look, I saw that one of the guarantors was an E. T. Werhan. As Werhan is a less common name than Porter, I went in search of E. T. Werhan.

The 1930 U.S. federal census had an Ed T. Werhan in Muskogee's Ward 3. The household he headed included wife, Grace; daughter, Dorothy; two nephews, Haskell and Gerald Porter; and Werhan's father-in-law, a man in his seventies named Thomas Jefferson Porter. The 1910 census had a T. Porter in the township of Ogle (in southwest Muskogee). In that household: Porter's sons Hal and Floyd, daughters Addie and Grace, and son-in-law E. T. "Wirehan."

And wonders never cease. I was fortunate to find a great-granddaughter of Thomas Jefferson Porter: Floyanne Porter Coursey of Sapulpa, Oklahoma. Floyanne and I could never prove that her T. J. Porter was the same man who had been one of Sarah's legal guardians, but the circumstantial evidence made us both smile. And she was good enough to share several old family photographs with me.

The man seated is Thomas Jefferson Porter. Seated near him is his wife, Rosa. This family photograph was taken in Muskogee, c. early 1900s.

GLOSSARY

Definitions of words and phrases are given relative to their use in this book.

allotment: Land assigned to a person.

as the crow flies: The shortest distance between two points, a route a bird might take because it doesn't have to deal with things on land, like mountains.

ballyhoo: Fanfare, hoopla, hype. Also, to push or promote something or someone by such means.

barrel of oil: Forty-two U.S. gallons.

black gold: Slang for crude oil (unrefined petroleum).

bond: An investment in debt, with the investor lending money to a public or private entity raising money for a project (building a bridge, for example). The "bondholder" lends the money for a certain period of time and for a fixed rate of interest. A "guardianship bond" is a form of insurance, with the guardian pledging a certain amount of money to his or her ward in the event that the guardian is found guilty of any wrongdoing in regard to the ward's estates.

boomtown: A town that grows rapidly because of sudden prosperity.

brouhaha: Uproar, hubbub.

claptrap: Absurd talk or thinking.

collateral: Something pledged (for instance, real estate or a diamond ring) to secure a loan. If the borrower doesn't repay the loan, the lender is entitled to keep the collateral.

court order: A command from a judge or group of judges.

Creek freedmen: Blacks who were made members of the Creek Nation after the Civil War. Most of them had been held in slavery by Creeks in I.T. They included both men and women, but all were called "freedmen."

crude oil: Unrefined petroleum.

Cushing-Drumright Field: One of the largest oil fields ever discovered in America. By 1915, it was producing roughly 300,000 barrels a day.

Department of the Interior: The part of the U.S. government that oversees the nation's natural resources. This department also administers programs for native peoples in the nation's states and territories.

depot: Train station.

derrick: A towerlike structure over an oil well.

doodad: A trinket, bauble, or gadget.

dry hole: A well with very little or no oil.

duster: Slang for dry hole.

estate: Someone's assets (including property, personal belongings, and money) as well as liabilities, such as debts.

first-mortgage loan: A loan in which real estate serves as collateral.

foreclose: To take possession of someone's property (usually real estate) after that person has failed to repay a loan for which the property was collateral.

Five Civilized Tribes: A designation whites gave five Indian nations from the Southeast—Cherokee, Chickasaw, Choctaw, Creek, and Seminole—because many members of these nations adopted Anglo-American ways. Many people who considered these Indians "civilized" considered other Indians "savages" because they did not adopt these ways. Today, many people prefer not to use the term "Five Civilized Tribes" because it upholds the notion that one culture is superior to others and is the touchstone of what it means to be civilized. Thus, instead of "Five Civilized Tribes," many people use the "Five Tribes" or the "Five Tribes of the Southeast."

Glenn Pool: An oil field in Oklahoma's Creek and Tulsa Counties. The discovery well was found on land owned by a Creek woman, Ida Glenn.

gold digger: A person who, with bad intentions, seeks a relationship with another person solely for material gain.

graft: Money or other profits gained by immoral means and the immoral use of one's position to enrich oneself or gain other benefits. A person who engages in graft is a "grafter."

grub: Slang for food.

gusher: An oil well from which oil jets up like a geyser (as opposed to having to be pumped up). A gusher indicates that there is a large reservoir of oil below the surface.

I.T.: Indian Territory. Land reserved primarily for Indians from the Southeast in the early nineteenth century. The territory was present-day Oklahoma without the panhandle.

interest: Money earned or paid on a loan. For example, if someone borrowed $5,000 from Sarah at 8 percent "simple interest" for three years, at the end of the loan Sarah would have been repaid $6,200. (Simple interest is money earned or paid on the original amount lent or put on deposit. With "compound interest" one earns or pays interest on the interest as well.)

lease: To rent, or a rental agreement.

landman: A person who works for an oil operator or oil company. A landman's services include brokering oil and gas leases.

legal guardian: A person approved by the court to manage financial and other important matters of someone incapable of handling his or her own affairs because that person is too young or incapacitated.

oil boom: A rapid rise in oil drilling and production.

petition: To make a formal request. Also, a document making a formal request.

pickaninny: A derogatory term for a black child.

pool: One or more large reservoirs of crude oil.

plute: Slang for a *plutocrat* or wealthy person. In ancient mythology, Pluto, god of the underworld, was also the god of riches.

probate: A process for establishing that a deceased person's will is genuine. Probate courts sometimes had jurisdiction over other matters as well, such as the estates of the living.

revenue: Income.

rig: The equipment used to drill an oil well, from the derrick to the drill.

river bottom land: Also known as "bottomland," it's land near a river. Its rich soil is ideal for farming.

scuttlebutt: Slang for gossip or rumor. On a ship, a scuttlebutt was a cask that held drinking water, the equivalent of an office watercooler around which people often chat and gossip.

signing bonus: A lump sum of money to induce a person to sign a contract. The money is payable upon signing the contract.

sovereignty: Independence, self-governance, autonomy, freedom.

spud in: To begin drilling a well.

tribe: A group of people who share common ancestry or culture.

tuberculosis: A contagious infection that primarily attacks the lungs.

Tuskegee: A city in Macon County, Alabama. Also a historically black institute, then university in the city of Tuskegee. The word comes from the Creek *taskiki*, meaning "warriors."

ward: Someone placed in the care of a guardian because of that person's youth or inability to handle his or her affairs.

wildcatter: An oil operator who drills for oil where none has been found within a mile or more.

NOTES

Unless otherwise noted, court petitions and orders are from the Muskogee County District Court, Probate No. 470. Some biographical data on Sarah and her family are taken from the 1900, 1910, 1920, and 1930 U.S. federal censuses, accessed via Ancestry.com. Additional information comes from their Dawes Packets.

A Dawes Packet is a file of information tied to an application for a land allotment in Indian Territory, which includes a birth affidavit, census cards, and often testimony. They are called Dawes Packets because they were assembled by the Department of the Interior's Commission to the Five Civilized Tribes, also known as the Dawes Commission. Headed by Massachusetts Senator Henry Dawes, the commission was in charge of the land allotment process.

I acquired Dawes Packets for Sarah and her family from the National Archives and Records Administration, Southwest Region, in Fort Worth, Texas, after providing Dawes census card and roll number information located through the U.S. Native American Enrollment Cards for the Five Civilized Tribes, 1898–1914, at Ancestry.com.

PROLOGUE

page 1 Melby's letter: "Find Sarah Rector," *Chicago Defender*, March 28, 1914, 8. John A. Melby is surely the architect John Alexander Melby, the second black person admitted to the University of Illinois School of Architecture (in 1899). Melby taught at Tuskegee Institute (1906–09).

page 1 "Where is Sarah Rector?": "Millionaire Colored Girl Kidnapped? Not at Tuskegee," *Chicago Defender*, March 14, 1914, 1.

page 1 money equivalent: here and throughout, the figure is determined by using the Purchasing Power Calculator at MeasuringWorth.com.

ONE: 160 ACRES

page 3 "hired hands": *Black Indian Slave Narratives*, 132.

page 7 "I remember my ... cultivated much land": *Indian-Pioneer Papers*, vol. 17, 215.

page 8 "Your white brothers ...": *Niles' Weekly Register*, June 13, 1829, 258.

pages 9, 10 grandfathers' Civil War service: *Civil War Pension Index: General Index to Pension Files, 1861–1934* at Ancestry.com and the McGilbra/Jackson pension file at National Archives, Washington, D.C. Prior to serving in the 2nd Kansas/83rd USCT,

John Rector may have served in the 1st Kansas. According to John Rector's Dawes Census Card, his original name was John McQueen, and there was a John McQueen who mustered in the 1st Kansas in May 1863 and who deserted a few weeks later. Correspondence from Blair Tarr, November 30, 2011.

page 14 Creek Nation enrollees for allotments by 1907: *The Dawes Commission*, 64.

TWO: THREE AND A HALF DOLLARS AN ACRE

page 15 early Taft: Gray, "Taft: Town on the Black Frontier," *The Chronicles of Oklahoma*, Winter 1988–89, 430–47.

page 16 sale of Mr. Rector's allotment: Telephone conversation with Robin Finch at Okmulgee Land Title Company, December 11, 2011.

page 18 taxes: "Guardian's Report," February 11, 1914.

page 18 Alvin: He is "Alfred" or "Alford" in some documents. Sarah's family provided his correct name and his date of birth (November 13, 1909). Correspondence from the ad hoc committee speaking on behalf of several Rector family members, December 10, 2010.

page 18 Joe Sr.'s guardianship: "Petition for Appointment of Guardian," January 14, 1909, and "Order Appointing Guardian," December 24, 1909.

page 18 sale of Rebecca's land: "Appraisal Before Sale of Lands at Private Sale," November 28, 1910 (which valued Rebecca's land at $640), and "Return of Sale of Real Estate," December 17, 1910.

page 20 oil production of the Glenn Pool: *Bulletin No. 19. Petroleum and Natural Gas in Oklahoma*, part 2, 186.

page 20 Devonian deal: "Return and Report of Guardian on Oil and Gas Mining Lease," February 21, 1911, and "Release," February 10, 1912.

page 20 petition to sell Sarah's land: "Petition to Sell Real Estate by Guardian," notarized March 18, 1912.

page 21 lease to Frank Barnes: "Guardian's Final Report of Execution of Oil and Gas Mining Lease," March 30, 1912.

page 21 Slick's strike on the Wheeler farm: *"King of the Wildcatters,"* 29–33.

page 21 Barnes's sale of lease to Jones: #8786 Assignment of Oil & Gas Lease, April 1, 1912, Creek County Register of Deeds.

page 22 Jones's possible investment: *"King of the Wildcatters,"* 28.

THREE: TWELVE AND A HALF PERCENT

page 23 date of Sarah's first gusher: "Report of Appraisers," April 6, 1918, 2.

page 23 "Little Sarah Will . . .": *Muskogee Times-Democrat*, September 4, 1913, 3.

page 23 ice cream soda: ad for Bereolos' Candy Kitchen, *Muskogee Times-Democrat*, July 3, 1913, 5.

page 24 "in the woods . . . and other expenses": "The Crisis in Oklahoma Indian Affairs: A Challenge to Our National Honor," *Report of the Thirty-Second Annual Lake Mohonk Conference of Friends of the Indian and Other Dependent Peoples, October 14, 15, and 16, 1914*, 18.

page 25 "The State Is After . . .": *Muskogee Times-Democrat*, April 7, 1910, 1, 4.

page 25 Durant twins and Burnett: "Barnett [*sic*] Gives Up," *Muskogee Times-Democrat*, July 27, 1911, 1; "New Guardians Wanted," *Muskogee Times-Democrat*, July 28, 1911, 8; "Guardian Litigation Is Settled at Last," *Muskogee Times-Democrat*, July 29, 1912, 2.

page 25 August 1914 fire: James, "Oil Storage," *The Quarterly*, January 1917, 264.

page 26 Sarah's new wells: "Gusher," *Muskogee Times-Democrat*, October 27, 1913, 1.

page 26 claims that Sarah was a full-blooded Indian and an orphan: untitled, *Clearfield [Pennsylvania] Progress*, December 14, 1915, 4, and "Negro Boy Gets $190 a Day," *Washington Post*, May 10, 1914, Miscellany Section, 3.

page 27 "Richest Colored Girl ... comforts for her": *Chicago Defender*, November 29, 1913, 1.

page 28 "Oil Made Pickaninny Rich": *Washington Post*, January 25, 1914, Miscellany Section, 3.

page 28 purchase of land for Sarah's new home: "Petition," December 29, 1913, and "Order," January 12, 1914. In all likelihood, construction on the house began before Leahy's court order.

page 28 "beds, bedding, chairs ...": "Petition," January 29, 1914. A court order allowing this was issued the same day.

page 28 Porter getting letters: "Oil Made Pickaninny Rich," *Washington Post*, January 25, 1914, Miscellany Section, 3.

page 28 Doggett letter: "Still Seeking Slices of Sarah Rector's Cash," *Muskogee Times-Democrat*, August 25, 1914, 3.

page 28 marriage proposals: "Young Germans Willing to Marry Sarah Rector, World's Richest Negro," *Muskogee-Times Democrat*, January 13, 1914, 1, 8.

page 29 "Constant protest and publicity ...": "Sarah Rector Is Not a Foreigner but an Afro-American," *Chicago Defender*, February 14, 1914, 6.

page 29 "a trick ... can not be hid": "Millionaire Colored Girl Kidnapped? Not at Tuskegee," *Chicago Defender*, March 14, 1914, 1.

page 30 "composed of ...": "Booker T. Washington," *Muskogee Cimeter*, November 23, 1905, 1.

page 30 "Here in the South ...": "Booker T. Washington in Muskogee," Muskogee History and Genealogy, Monday October 1, 2007, muskogeehistorian.com.

page 31 Stella and Herbert Sells: The ages of the children varied from paper to paper. According to Stella's birth affidavit, she was born April 3, 1901. According to the 1900 U.S. Federal Census, Herbert was born in October 1897. In some sources, Stella is "Castella" and "Costella." Among the articles on the Sells tragedy are: "House Blown Up; Children Killed," *Daily Oklahoman*, March 24, 1911, 2; "Taft Dynamiting Case Is Called," *Muskogee Times-Democrat*, December 11, 1911, 1; " 'Doc' Allen Confessed," *Cherokee*

Republican, December 28, 1911, 1; "Muskogee Man Guilty," *Checotah Times*, December 29, 1911, 4; "A Jury Is Selected to Try F. L. Martin," *Muskogee Times-Democrat*, December 30, 1911, 1; and "Negro Father Is Held for Murder," *Daily Oklahoman*, February 13, 1912, 4.

page 31 Zeb Mackey's acquittal: "Mackey Discharged," *Daily Oklahoman*, March 9, 1912, 3. Some sources say that Zeb Mackey was guilty of killing his stepchildren, but I found no record of his being convicted in a court of law for this.

page 31 Sarah not missing: "Little Sarah Rector Found; Suitors Seek Her," *Chicago Defender*, April 4, 1914, 1.

page 32 "has been exceptionally . . .": "Letter from State of Oklahoma to James C. Waters Jr., June 2, 1914."

page 32 Leahy's letter: "Letter from County Court of Muskogee County Muskogee, Oklahoma to W. E. B. Du Bois, June 11, 1914."

FOUR: ONE MILLION DOLLARS

page 33 Sarah's money and living conditions: "Letter from County Court of Muskogee County Muskogee, Oklahoma to W.E.B. Du Bois, June 11, 1914.

page 36 Mr. Rector's resignation and nomination and appointment of Porter: "Petition of Guardian Tendering His Resignation," notarized July 25,

1913; "Nomination of Father and Mother for Appointment of Guardian," notarized July 26, 1913; and "Order Accepting Resignation [of] Joe Rector and Appointing T. J. Porter as Guardian of Said Wards," July 26, 1913. Porter also became Rebecca's and Joe Jr.'s guardian. I found no evidence that their estates ever amounted to much.

page 36 Porter's compensation and services: "Petition" and "Order," January 29, 1914. Porter applied for compensation six months after he became Sarah's guardian. His services included, through his attorney, Edward Curd Jr., suing the state of Oklahoma on Sarah's behalf. Sarah's estate became part of the famous "riverbed" cases. Oklahoma had maintained that it owned the waterways even if they crossed someone's land. In Sarah's case, the government had leased the rights to drill in a stream that cut through her land to a company owned by Charles Haskell, a former Oklahoma governor. Porter sued for Sarah to get 12.5 percent of the oil Haskell's company brought in. It would take a while, but in the end the lawsuit was successful (*Rector v. United States et al.*, No. 7172, Circuit Court of Appeals, Eighth Circuit, May 28, 1927).

page 36 guardians' fees: *The American Indian in the United States: Period 1850–1914*, 155.

page 36 4 percent interest: "Petition," January 29, 1914.

page 36 Mr. Rector's allowance: In his letter to Du Bois, Judge Leahy said Sarah's father was getting $50 per month. He misspoke. A few days before he replied to Du Bois, Leahy had increased the allowance to $65, effective June 1. ("Order," May 28, 1914.)

page 37 "honest" and "a terror": "Judge Thos. W. Leahy," *Haskell News*, July 30, 1914, 1; and untitled in second column, *Haskell News*, June 18, 1914, 4.

page 37 "It takes an awful . . .": "Echo! Three Cheers for Judge Leahy," *Muskogee Cimeter*, September 2, 1911, 1.

page 39 Sarah's "comforts": "Order," February 4, 1914 (phonograph); "Order," May 28, 1914 (piano); "Order," April 19, 1917 (three rooms); "Petition," notarized July 30, 1917, and "Order," August 7, 1917 (garage); "Order," July 6, 1917 (Premier); "Order," June 27, 1918 (Cadillac).

page 41 on June 11 law: *Reports of the Department of the Interior*, Vol. 2., 272–73.

page 42 bills: April and September 1917 statements attached to "Petition to Pay Accounts," October 6, 1917.

page 42 gold watch: "Order," February 12, 1918.

page 42 Sarah and Rebecca at Tuskegee: correspondence from Cheryl Ferguson at the Tuskegee Archive, March 14, 2011.

page 42 Prairie Oil and Gas bonus: "Return and Report of Guardians on Oil and Gas Mining Lease," April 30, 1918.

page 42 Sarah's farmland in Muskogee and Wagoner Counties: "Guardians' Reports for First Half of 1919" for January 1919–June 30, 1919, and "Final Report of Guardians" for January 20, 1920–March 2, 1920. Sarah also had farmland in Haskell County.

page 42 Sarah's building on South Second Street: "Information Relative to Fike Building Owned by Robert H. Fike," no date. The October 1915 *Crisis* (p. 279) reprinted a piece the black-owned *Tulsa Star* ran a few months earlier in which it said that the Fike building was a "white elephant" and that Sarah's estate had paid an "extortionate" price for it. In its October 23, 1915, issue, however, the *Tulsa Star* stepped back from its original position and called Sarah's building one of "two valuable pieces of Muskogee." According to a document cited above, in 1914 the building and the ground on which it stood was assessed at $41,000, and assessments for the purpose of property taxes are always below a property's market value. This document also stated that the net annual income from the building (that is, the income after taxes and other expenses were deducted) was a little over $5,000.

page 43 $1 million: "Petition for Appointment of Guardian," February 10, 1920, 1.

page 44 November 3, 1916, hearing: "Hearing on Petition to Purchase 514.14 acres Real Estate in Muskogee and Wagoner Counties, Oklahoma," November 3, 1916, 1–8, 10.

EPILOGUE

page 46 nomination of Mr. Rector and Porter as guardians: "Nomination of Sarah Rector of Guardian," October 30, 1916 (notarized in Davidson County, Tennessee). According to several court documents, Sarah and Rebecca were at the time in Nashville, attending the historically black university Fisk, no doubt its preparatory school. Fisk does not have student records from back then (correspondence from Beth Howse, Special Collections, June 15, 2011). Among court documents that refer to Sarah being in Tennessee and/or attending Fisk is a May 1917 Porter-Young petition to spend $350 of Sarah's money for school expenses and railroad fare for her to be brought home from school for the summer. They stated that "their ward is attending school with her sister at Fisk University, Nashville, Tenn."

page 46 proposed Porter-Rector guardianship: "Hearing on Nomination of Ward T. J. Porter and Joe Rector, as Guardians," November 24, 1916, and "Motion to Withdraw Nomination of Sarah Rector as to Joe Rector from the Files," December 21, 1916.

page 46 Young as co-guardian: "Nomination of Sarah Rector," December 21, 1916; "Waiver," December 21, 1916; "Order Appointing Guardian," December 22, 1916; and "Letters of Guardianship," December 28, 1916.

page 46 Sarah having an account at Young's bank: "Guardian's Report" for February 10, 1916, to August 5, 1916.

page 47 Porter's resignation: "Resignation of T. J. Porter, as Guardian," August 18, 1917, and "Rector Guardian Quits Under Fire," *Muskogee Times-Democrat*, August 18, 1917, 1.

page 47 Looney becoming co-guardian: "Letters of Guardianship," September 5, 1917.

page 47 Curd's wrongdoing: *State ex rel. Dale et al., State Bar com'rs, v. Curd,* 1919.

page 47 suit against Curd: "Attorney Sued for Double Fee," *Muskogee Times-Democrat*, August 1, 1919, 12, and "Final Report of Guardians," March 1920.

page 47 probe and Jefferson's suspension: "Guardianship Probe Ends in Big Sensation," *Muskogee Times-Democrat*, November, 24, 1917, 1, and "Bar Jefferson from Practice," *Muskogee-Times Democrat*, August 31, 1920, 1.

page 47 Sarah's freedom from guardianship: "Needs No Guardian," *Star Journal* (Sandusky, Ohio), March 21, 1922, 1.

page 47 Sarah's spending and investments: "Sarah Rector—Kansas City's First Black Millionairess," *Kansas City Call*, February 15, 1991, 1, 12, and "Sarah Rector (Campbell)," *An Extraordinary Man*.

page 48 Sarah's marriage to Kenneth Campbell: State of Kansas, Central Division of Vital Statistics Marriage License C No. 11537. Sarah and Kenneth married in Lawrence, Kansas, on September 19, 1922. The license lists them as both being nineteen years old.

page 49 death of Sarah's father: Texas State Board of Health, Bureau of Vital Statistics, Standard Certificate of Death.

page 49 Sarah's marriage to William Crawford and her death and burial: Funeral Program and Missouri Division of Health—Standard Certificate of Death.

page 49 Sale of allotment: General Warranty Deed, Creek County, recorded in Book 274, page 6.

page 49 Sarah's land in Oklahoma by 1933: correspondence from Guaranty Abstract Company in Stigler, Oklahoma; Wagoner County Abstract Company; and Pioneer Abstract & Title Company in Muskogee, Oklahoma.

page 49 Sarah's oil wells by 1933 and beyond: correspondence from the Oklahoma Corporation Commission.

page 50 "a very private person": "Sarah Rector—Kansas City's First Black Millionairess," *Kansas City Call*, February 15, 1991, 12.

AUTHOR'S NOTE

page 52 Mr. Rector knowing Porter for seven or eight years: "Hearing on Petition to Purchase Real Estate," November 4, 1916.

page 52 E. T. Werhan and T. J. Porter connection: "Township Officers," *Muskogee Times-Democrat*, September 3, 1907, 6; "Old Board Is Not Worrying," *Muskogee-Times Democrat*, June 9, 1913, 6; and "Guardian's Bond," July 26, 1913.

SELECTED SOURCES

Barnard, Kate. "The Crisis in Oklahoma Indian Affairs: A Challenge to Our National Honor," *Report of the Thirty-Second Annual Lake Mohonk Conference of the Indian and Other Dependent Peoples, October 14, 15, and 16, 1914*. Mohonk Lake, N.Y.: Lake Mohonk Conference on the Indian and Other Dependent Peoples, 1914.

Buchanan, Jas. S. "Interview with Fannie Rentie Chapman," *Indian-Pioneer Papers*, vol. 17, 214–17. University of Oklahoma Libraries Western History Collections. Online.

Carter, Kent. *The Dawes Commission and the Allotment of the Five Civilized Tribes, 1893–1914*. Orem, Utah: Ancestry.com, 1999.

Cruce, Lee. "Letter from State of Oklahoma to James C. Waters Jr., June 2, 1914," credo.library.umass.edu.

Debo, Angie. *And Still the Waters Run: The Betrayal of the Five Civilized Tribes*. Norman: University of Oklahoma Press, 1984. Originally published in 1940.

———. *The Road to Disappearance: A History of the Creek Indians*. Norman: University of Oklahoma Press, 1979. Originally published in 1941.

Department of the Interior. *Reports of the Department of the Interior*, vol. 2. Washington, D.C.: Government Printing Office, 1915.

Foreman, Grant. *The Five Civilized Tribes: Cherokee, Chickasaw, Choctaw, Creek, Seminole*. Norman: University of Oklahoma Press, 1971. Originally published in 1934.

Goins, Charles Robert, and Danney Globe. *Historical Atlas of Oklahoma*, 4th ed. Norman: University of Oklahoma Press, 2006.

Gray, Linda C. "Taft: Town on the Black Frontier," *Chronicles of Oklahoma*, vol. 66, no. 4 (Winter 1988–89), 430–47.

James, Garrett B. "Oil Storage," *Quarterly of the National Fire Protection Association*, January 1917.

Johnson, Hannibal B. *Acres of Aspiration: The All-Black Towns in Oklahoma*. Austin: Eakin Press, 2002.

Jones, Carmen. "Sarah Rector—Kansas City's First Black Millionairess," *Kansas City Call*, February 15, 1991, 1, 12.

Krumme, George. "The Jones Family," *Bristow News*, seven installments, from June 27 to August 8, 2012, 7.

Leahy, Thomas W. "Letter from County Court of Muskogee County, Muskogee, Oklahoma, to W. E. B. Du Bois, June 11, 1914," credo.library.umass.edu.

Miles, Ray. *"King of the Wildcatters": The Life and Times of Tom Slick, 1883–1930*. College Station: Texas A&M University Press, 2004.

Minges, Patrick, ed. *Black Indian Slave Narratives*. Winston-Salem: John F. Blair, 2004.

Moorehead, Warren K. *The American Indian in the United States, Period 1850–1914*. Andover, Mass.: Andover Press, 1914.

Patton, Stacey. "The Richest Colored Girl in the World," the *Crisis*, Spring 2010, 31–34.

Perdue, Theda, and Michael D. Green. *The Columbia Guide to American Indians of the Southeast*. New York: Columbia University Press, 2001.

Restuccia, B. S. "Rusty," with E. Edward "Sonny" Gibson and Geraldlyn "Geri" Sanders. *An Extraordinary Man: Homer B. Roberts, 1885–1952*. Ann Arbor: Rustic Enterprise, 2001.

Shannon, C. W., et al. *Bulletin No. 19. Petroleum and Natural Gas in Oklahoma*, part 2. Norman: Oklahoma Geological Survey, April 1917.

Unrau, William E. *The Rise and Fall of Indian Country, 1825–1855*. Lawrence: University Press of Kansas, 2007.

Zellar, Gary. *African Creeks: Estelvste and the Creek Nation*. Norman: University of Oklahoma Press, 2007.

ACKNOWLEDGMENTS

Thank you, Sherelle Harris, for planting the seed.

Thank you, my editor, Howard Reeves, for believing in this book when I had little information and for those magic words after I gathered more information than I knew what to do with at first.

Thanks also to other tremendous talents with Abrams: editorial assistants Jenna Pocius and Melissa Faulner; managing editor James Armstrong; copyeditor Phyllis DeBlanche; fact-checker David Webster; proofreader Rob Sternitzky; associate art director Maria Middleton; associate production director Alison Gervais; children's marketing and publicity manager Laura Mihalick; and marketing and publicity director Jason Wells.

And there were friends who read different drafts or let me pick their brains on particular matters, or both: Elza Dinwiddie-Boyd, writer and educator, born and raised in Taft, Oklahoma; Jacqueline Gantt Brathwaite, New York City school librarian; Rodney Brisco, Texas attorney with expertise in the oil industry; Susan Hess, New York City school librarian; Sandra Karreim, lawyer; Kim Pearson, civic media researcher and educator; Jim Shepard, investment strategist. I am also grateful to the Bronx, New York, Teaching American History triumvirate: Brian Carlin, Marsha Green, and Philip Panaritis, for the fine feedback on an early draft.

Bless you, Angela Y. Walton-Raji, author, educator, genealogist, researcher, and Choctaw freedman descendant, for reading copy, for procuring some documents from the National Archives in D.C., and for so freely and generously sharing your knowledge about I.T. history. The universe thanks you for your blog: *The African—Native American Genealogy Blog*.

I am also grateful to two women whose work on Sarah preceded mine. Thank you, Geraldlyn R. Sanders, for taking questions; for providing copies of Lillie Rector's death certificate, Sarah and Kenneth's marriage license, Sarah's death certificate, Sarah's funeral program, a few articles I did not have; for information on William Crawford's restaurant; but most of all for overall insights on Sarah's Kansas City days and for reading an early draft of the epilogue and providing valuable commentary, corrections, and confirmations on it. Thank you, Stacey Patton, for the lively exchanges.

Beth Howse at Fisk Special Collections and Danielle Kovacks at the University of Massachusetts, Amherst Special Collections: It was such a pleasure to work with you both again. Cheryl Ferguson at Tuskegee University Archives: So great dealing with you for the first time.

This book had many other angels: people who took my inquiries seriously, so many of them in Oklahoma. In the beginning there was Linda Garrison, deputy clerk at the Muskogee County District Court. Had you not taken my initial inquiry seriously, I may well have abandoned the project. Thanks for going above and beyond. Other Muskogee angels: Nancy Calhoun and the entire staff at Muskogee Public Library's Genealogy and Local History department; Suzanne Jobe, Pioneer Abstract and Title Company; and Wally Waits, historian and genealogist.

I am also grateful to so many others elsewhere in the Sooner State.

In Bristow: June Hurst at the Montfort and Allie B. Jones Memorial Library.

In Norman: Jacquelyn Slater and Jacquelyn Sparks, Western History Collections, University of Oklahoma Libraries.

In Oklahoma City: Donna K. Darnell, Manager, Oil & Gas Complaints & Information, Consumer Services Division, Oklahoma Corporation Commission, and Terry Grooms, also with the OCC, for referring me to Donna the Undaunted—and so diligent! Other Oklahoma City angels: Beverly Mosman and Larry O'Dell, Research Division, Oklahoma Historical Society, Oklahoma History Center; Lori Oden, Oklahoma Museum of History, Oklahoma Historical Society, Oklahoma History Center; Kathy

Smith, Office of the Oklahoma Secretary of State; and Jim Rabon, Oklahoma Department of Corrections.

In Okmulgee: Robin Finch, Okmulgee Land Title Company.

In Sapulpa: Floyanne Moore Coursey; Sandie Howard, Creek County Clerk; and Sherry Tobias, Union-Creek Abstract Company.

In Stigler: Ramona Forrester, Guaranty Abstract & Title Company.

In Tulsa: Dr. George Krumme, oilman and writer, who read the final draft carefully enough to catch some errors.

In Wagoner: Linda Greer, Wagoner County Abstract Company.

Outside of Oklahoma, there were angels, too: Apryle Brown, Kansas City, Missouri, School District; Jeremy Drouin and Shannon Julien, Kansas City Public Library's Missouri Valley Special Collections; Stuart Hinds, Miller Nichols Library, UMKC; Ray Miles, author of *"King of the Wildcatters"*; Denise Morrison, Union Station, Kansas City; Theda Perdue, University of North Carolina, Chapel Hill; Blair D. Tarr, museum curator, Kansas State Historical Society in Topeka, Kansas; and Gary Zellar, author of *African Creeks*.

Last but not least, Sarah Rector's family. My initial contact was with Paula Rector Davis, who heard me out in that first phone call, then opened the door to the rest of the "family committee." Bless you, Paula, and you, too, Deborah Brown; Diann Brown; Sarah Campbell; John Edwards; Lillian Gibbs; Roy E. Gibbs Jr.; Rosina Graves; Rashonda Duncan Lunnie; Joseph Rector, III; Toni Gibbs Rowe; and Donna Brown Thompkins. It's no small thing to have a stranger poking around in your family history, and so I am ever grateful for your e-mail time, your phone time, your searching time, your remembering time.

ILLUSTRATION CREDITS

INDEX

Note: Page numbers in italics refer to illustrations.